Fuzzy theories on decision-making

Frontiers in Systems Research:
Implications for the social sciences

Vol. 3

The objective of the series is to develop a rich resource of advanced literature devoted to the implications of systems research for the social sciences. The series includes monographs and collections of articles suitable for graduate students and researchers in academia and business, including rewritten Ph. D. dissertations. No undergraduate textbooks or reference books are included. Quality, originality and relevance with respect to the objectives of the series will be used as primary criteria for accepting submitted manuscripts.

Fuzzy theories on decision-making

A critical review

Walter J. M. Kickert

Eindhoven University of Technology

Martinus Nijhoff Social Sciences Division
Leiden/Boston/London 1978

Sole distributors for North America:
Kluwer Boston Inc.,
160 Old Derby Street
Hingham, Ma.

ISBN 90.207.0760.4

Printed in the Netherlands.

0

Foreword

Fuzzy set theory is a research area that is growing at an incredible speed. Contrary to common practice in forewords I shall not sketch the beautiful perspectives nor the brilliant future of the subject, for it is the urgent need for a realistic, sober assessment of the theory's usefulness that has induced me to write this book. Although it is completely understandable that the supporters of such a brand-new theory should support their theory in the most convincing way possible, this support sometimes appears rather overdone. I think the time has come to start an honest evaluation in order to stimulate the right development of the subject. Hopefully this book will be a contribution to that end.

I am very grateful to Professors J. G. Dijkman, B. R. Gaines and H. J. Zimmermann for their critical and helpful comments on earlier versions of the manuscript and for their encouragement. As a matter of course this does not imply that they are to be held responsible for my opinions displayed throughout the book. Fortunately I know that they share some of these opinions.

Walter J. M. Kickert
Eindhoven, January 1978

Contents

List of symbols

μ	fuzzy membership function
$\in$	is element of
$\notin$	is not element of
$\subset$	is subset of
$\cup$	union
$\cap$	intersection
$\overline{A}$	complementation
$\neg A$	complementation
$\varnothing$	empty set
$A \times B$	cartesian product of A and B
card (A)	number of elements of A
$\rightarrow$	mapping
$\vee$	disjunction (maximum)
$\wedge$	conjunction (minimum)
$\Rightarrow$	implication
$\Leftrightarrow$	equivalence
iff	if and only if
$\therefore$	conclusion
$\exists x$	there exists an x
$\forall x$	for all x
$R_1 o R_2$	composition of relations R_1 and R_2
R	real numbers
R^+	positive real numbers
R^n	product of n sets of real numbers
$[a, b]$	closed interval $a \leq x \leq b$

Introduction

It is undeniable that decision-making is one of the major subjects of interest in the social sciences and that it is also one of the few fields in social science where applied mathematics have been able to contribute to the development of 'hard' theories. As with most mathematical theories about social systems, there seems to be a great disadvantage in the mathematical modelling of decision-making, namely the required (or imposed) precision underlying the model. Although probabilistic decision-theories and game theory claim to model decision-making under risk and under uncertainty, our idea is that there is a qualitatively different kind of uncertainty which is not covered by these theories – that is inexactness, ill-definedness, vagueness, or in short: fuzziness. Many situations occur where the notion of probability alone is not adequate to describe reality. Situations where doubt arises about the exactness of concepts, correctness of statements and judgements, degrees of credibility, and so on, have little to do with probability of occurrence, the fundamental concept of the probabilistic framework.

The aim of this book is to discuss the contribution of the theory of fuzziness, known as the fuzzy set theory, to the development of decision-making models.

Fuzzy set theory was originated by · L. A. Zadeh in 1965 as a mathematical theory of vagueness (Zadeh 1965a). Since then the research on fuzzy sets has steadily increased up to the present stage where some hundreds of papers on the subject appear every year (Gaines and Kohout 1977). It is, however, quite understandable that many scientists are still fairly sceptical of this new theory. Though the majority of papers start by emphasising the usefulness of the theory to all kinds of complex social systems, most do not justify these claims of applicability. Honestly speaking, it appears absolutely impossible for any theory, whatever it may be, to satisfy such universal claims as:

'Such methods could open new frontiers in psychology, sociology, social

science, philosophy, economics, linguistics, operations research, management science and other fields and provide a basis for the design of systems far superior in artificial intelligence than those we can conceive today' (preface by Zadeh in Kaufmann 1973, p. vii).
though L. A. Zadeh himself has contributed tremendously to the advancement of fuzzy systems theory.

An example of a sceptical scientist is M. A. Arbib who gave some serious criticisms in his recent book reviews. In his opinion the fuzzy set research presented in the three books that he has reviewed, could be pictured as follows:

'There is little ... of purely mathematical interest'.

'Much of the work is philosophically naive'.

'The applications suffer from being contributions to fuzzy set theory ... rather than contributions to decision theory, or pattern recognition, or whatever' (Arbib 1977, p. 950).

Although it is a pity that Arbib himself seems to be more interested in pure mathematics than in practical applications, and some of his remarks seem to be a bit overdone, his last point alas makes sense. In spite of the frequent and rather general claims of applicability, little research on fuzzy sets is oriented to the solution of practical problems and indeed the impression is created that some existing practical examples are sought out to show the abilities of fuzzy set theory rather than that these examples originated from acute problems in the field of application.

This apparent lack of application-oriented fuzzy set research was my main reason for writing this book.

The best proof of the applicability of fuzzy set theory is to apply the theory and show its success. This surely has been done, will continue to be done, and it is the intention of the author to do so as well. In this book, however, we will try to evaluate the applicability of fuzzy sets to the field of decision-making by giving a critical survey of fuzzy research in that area – that is, by reviewing existing fuzzy theories on decision-making. Another argument which shows the need of a coherent survey of a particular field of application is the fact that fuzzy set research is carried out in numerous scattered areas. A short look at abstracts from congresses and symposia will prove this. There seems to be no coherence in the research: everyone is doing something different. A very pragmatic reason for the choice of the particular field of decision-making is the absolute impossibility of making a survey of the whole of fuzzy set research, simply because of the overwhelming quantity of existing literature. Global surveys are already available in the form of extensive bibliographies (Gaines and Kohout 1977), or in the form of several books which cover some important areas (Kaufmann 1973, 1975a, 1975b, 1977; Negoita and Ralescu 1975; Zadeh et al. 1975).

The final choice for decision-making was made because of the above-mentioned importance of the subject and because this seems a very promising field of application of fuzzy sets.

The emphasis on the applicability of the various fuzzy theories on decision-making implies that the fuzzy theories will be approached from the point of view of decision-making and not the other way round, herewith avoiding the above cited criticism. This has resulted in an accentuation of the relationships between these theories and conventional theories on decision-making. The partition of fuzzy theories that has been adopted in this book has therefore been guided by the usual classification of decision theories.

In Part One we will focus on fuzzy theories about one-stage decision-making. This is the part which is closest to conventional theories. Chapter 1 discusses the fuzzy counterpart to normative individual decision theory. Chapter 2 describes a decision model orientated more towards operations research, namely mathematical programming. In Chapter 3 we will discuss theories about multi-person decision-making. The last chapter of Part One discusses the field of multi-criteria decision-making.

The second part of the book will be devoted to multi-stage decision-making. In Chapter 5 the fuzzy extension of dynamic programming will be presented. Chapter 6 will discuss briefly the general concept of a fuzzy system. Chapter 7 discusses the linguistic modelling approach to decision processes.

This report is written for people interested in the usefulness and applicability of fuzzy set theory, particularly to decision-making. This implies that we shall not pay much attention to the more abstract, algebraic contributions. In order to make this book self-contained, an appendix is added in which the basic definitions of fuzzy set theory are introduced. This book should therefore be readable for people with a basic knowledge of decision theory and with some elementary mathematical training.

This introduction would not be complete if we did not mention the restrictions of the book. First of all we would like to apologise to those fuzzy set researchers who fail to find their contributions. We cannot claim to have reviewed all literature on fuzzy decision-making and have mainly restricted ourselves to officially published literature. Secondly, it should be emphasised that we cannot claim to have discussed the applicability of fuzzy set theory to decision-making in social systems. This would have required an approach from a social science point of view, while we shall discuss mainly mathematical theories. In addition, discussions about applicability in general would involve a methodological discussion. We will only touch on these points in the epilogue of the book.

It is our hope that this book will contribute to a more balanced judgement of the usefulness of fuzzy set theory in the sense that over-optimism may be moderated a little and over-scepticism refuted a little. Hopefully the book will have a stimulating effect on the development of application-orientated fuzzy set research.

Part One

One-stage decision-making

One-stage decision-making

As stated in the introduction, we shall here describe some existing fuzzy theories about non-sequential decision-making as far as they are related to the usual (mathematical) theories about decision-making. From a broad point of view almost every action results from a decision, so that almost every theory which involves taking action would be a decision theory. Although in principle a survey should be as broad as possible, in practice this is often impossible. Therefore we have had to restrict ourselves: only theories which were 'decision theories' in the conventional sense have been considered. The operational definition of a 'decision theory' which we have adopted is that the theory should incorporate some minimisation of a cost function (or maximisation of a utility function).

It will be clear that the importance of this area guarantees that there exist a lot of mathematical theories about decision-making. We shall try to glance through them quickly, firstly from the point of view of the application area, secondly from the point of view of the implied mathematics.

If we look at the application areas of the theories, they may be classified by easy-to-recognise dimensions such as the number of decision-makers involved, the number of stages before the decision is reached, the amount of vagueness encountered, and so on (Figure 1).

Along the axis 'number of decision-makers' – which incidentally do not have to be individuals – one might state that the statistical decision theory covers single person decision-making, while two-person decision-making is covered by two-person game theory, and multi-person decision-making by n-person game theory and the theory about collective decision-making (Luce and Raiffa 1957).

Multi-stage decision-making is covered by theories like dynamic programming and more generally by dynamic systems theory. Although these theories are extended to cope with uncertainty, combinations of multi-person and multi-stage decision-making are not extensively covered by any mathematical decision theory; some dynamisation of game theory exists and there is also a theory of conflict which amounts to non-linear differential equations (Boulding 1962). Multi-stage decision-making will be considered later in part two of this book. In the first part we shall restrict ourselves to theories where the decision is supposed to be taken in one step.

The axis 'amount of vagueness' corresponds to the usual tripartition into:

1. certainty: all information is deterministic; decision-making consists of a straightforward optimisation of a utility function.
2. risk: the information is probabilistic, only probability density functions are known; decision-making involves an optimisation of expected utility.
3. uncertainty: even probabilities are unknown; decision-making comes down to a minimax strategy to ensure the highest utility in the worst circumstances.

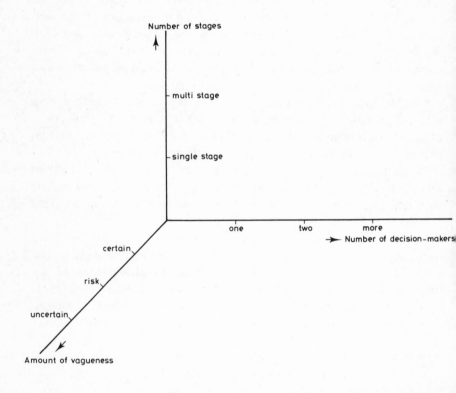

Fig. 1. Classification of decision theories.

It will be clear that fuzzy theories on decision-making should offer relief along this axis; for vagueness which not only concerns the occurrence of an event but the event itself is not dealt with by probabilistic methods. Here fuzziness should have a part to play.

A second way of classifying existing mathematical theories on one-stage decision-making is by looking at the essential mathematical contents of each class of theories. We might then arrive at the following four categories:

− decision-making viewed as an optimisation of expected utility.
− decision-making viewed as an optimisation under constraints.
− multi-person optimisation.
− multi-criteria optimisation.

This division is very pragmatic since it amounts to a division into the best-known and best-elaborated mathematical decision theories. Roughly speaking, the correspondencies between these four categories and the well-known conventional decision theories are as outlined in table 1.

Table 1. Classification of one-stage decision theories.

Category	Corresponding conventional theories	Dealt with in Chapter
Maximisation of expected utility	Statistical decision theory	One
Optimisation under constraints	Mathematical programming	Two
Multi-person optimisation	Game theory Collective decision-making	Three
Multi-criteria optimisation	Multi-criteria decision-making	Four

It is this classification that we have adopted in this part of the book in order to show most clearly the correspondencies between conventional mathematical decision theories and fuzzy theories on decision-making.

The first two classes are characterised by the fact that there is only one decision-maker (either an individual or an abstract decision-making entity), while for the third class the number of decision-makers is greater. The last class is also characterised by a single decision-maker, but here the alternatives cannot be ranked according to only one aspect: more aspects have to be incorporated into the final choice.

It should be remarked that in engineering literature most attention is paid to the second class of non-sequential decision-making, namely the 'optimisation under constraints' category, which is obviously the operations research type of decision-making. This fact is also reflected in literature on fuzzy decision-making (Negoita and Ralescu 1975, Kaufmann 1975b). We consider this to be only a restricted part of the area of decision theories.

1. Fuzzy individual decision-making

1.1. Introduction

It seems reasonable to consider first the well-known classical model of individual decision-making – the model of man as a *homo economicus* – where the decision-maker strives for maximisation of his (expected) utility. This model in fact forms the basis of all mathematical theories on decision-making.

In this chapter we will start by presenting this classical model of decision-making, especially that part of the model which forms its essence: the utility function. This deterministic model will then be extended to a fuzzy version. Thereafter we will introduce the probabilistic version of the classical model – well known as statistical decision theory – and show how fuzzy set theory can be applied to that version of the model.

1.2. The *homo economicus* model

In the classical model of decision-making the situation is supposed to be characterized by a set of alternative states (outcomes, results):

$$X = \{x_1 \ldots x_n\}.$$

The decision-maker can choose from a set of alternative actions:

$$A = \{a_1 \ldots a_m\}.$$

Furthermore it is known which action will lead to which outcome, in other words, there exists a relation:

$$R \subset A \times X$$

which indicates that if $(a_i, x_j) \in R$, then x_j will be the effect of action a_i. Finally the decision-maker possesses a preference ordering over all possible outcomes:

$$O \subset X \times X$$

This preference ordering can be represented by a value function $V(x_j)$. In this model the decision-maker will decide to take that action a_i which gives him the highest outcome value $V(x_j)$ where $(a_i, x_j) \in R$.

Note that this is a very simple version of the model. The relation might well be dependent on the present state. In that case the relation is a function, R then becomes:

$$R : A_t \times X_t \to X_{t+1}.$$

This is still a deterministic relation. Moreover the action-result relation might not be deterministic but e.g. probabilistic. The relation then becomes a probability distribution $P_{ij} = p(x_j | a_i)$ and the decision-maker will choose that value a_i which maximizes the expected value:

$$E(V) = \sum_j p(x_j | a_i) \, V(x_j)$$

It is this type of decision situation which is called decision-making under *risk*, whilst the deterministic case is called decision-making under *certainty*. The case where each action has a set of possible outcomes but where the probabilities of these outcomes are unknown is called decision-making under *uncertainty*. We come back to this later on in this chapter.

It will be clear that the 'value function' $V(x_j)$ plays an essential role in this model. Therefore we will pay some attention to it.

Utility function

In order to actually be able to take decisions with the above-mentioned model, there are some necessary requirements to be made to the preference ordering over the alternative states. Especially in the case of decision-making under risk. This has led to an axiomatic treatment resulting in the utility function theory. (Von Neumann and Morgenstern 1944; Fishburn 1964, 1970).

In words the axiomatic treatment of the preference ordering comes down to the following requirements (Luce and Raiffa 1957)
– all alternatives have to be comparable with each other (preference or indifference);
– preference and indifference are transitive relations;
– if a lottery has a lottery as an alternative, it can be decomposed into basic alternatives by means of probability calculus;
– if two lotteries are indifferent, they can be exchanged in a composed lottery;

– if two lotteries have the same two alternatives, the lottery in which the preferred alternative has the highest chance will be preferred;
– if x_i is preferred to x_j, and x_j to x_k, there exists a lottery with x_i and x_k which is indifferent to x_j.

A lottery is defined as a chance mechanism with probabilities $p_1(x_1)\ldots p_m(x_m)$ that alternatives $x_1\ldots x_m$ will occur ($\Sigma p_i = 1$).

This axiomatic system leads to the existence of a real-valued function φ on X so that:
– x_i is preferred to x_j if and only if (iff) $\varphi(x_i) > \varphi(x_j)$
– the value of the combination of x_i with probability α, and x_j with probability $1 - \alpha$, is the sum of α times the value of x_i, plus $1 - \alpha$ times the value of x_j:

$$\varphi(\alpha, x_i; 1 - \alpha, x_j) = \alpha\varphi(x_i) + (1 - \alpha)\varphi(x_j)$$

– if two functions φ and ψ satisfy these requirements, then:

$$\psi(x_i) = b\varphi(x_i) + c \qquad\qquad b, c \in R, b > 0.$$

This function is called the utility function. Note that the last conclusion means that the utility function is unique apart from zero and unity, that is, the function has interval-scale properties. There exists a lot of criticism of this utility function theory. In psychological experiments it often appears that the behaviour of individual decision-makers does not satisfy several underlying axioms of the utility function. In many situations the preference ordering of an individual is shown not even to be transitive. The explanation of this is often sought in the multi-dimensionality of the properties which determine the value judgement of a person.

In economics utility functions have mainly been criticised because of their interval-scale properties. Roughly speaking the interval-scale conclusion is implied by the requirement of additivity. In economic terms this means that the total utility of several commodities should be an additive function of the utilities of the separate commodities. Especially with non-independent utilities this has been shown to be not necessarily true. This kind of criticism has led to the development of alternatives to the utility function, of which indifference curves are an example. In order to be able to deal with non-independent utilities the notion of an indifference curve, which is a constant-utility curve for a combination of commodities, has been introduced. Take the classical example of bananas and apples and suppose that 10 apples plus 1 banana gives you the same utility as 6 apples plus 4 bananas (see Figure 2). Then these two points are on a indifference curve. Of course the indifference curve formed by e.g. 15 apples plus 5 bananas and 5 apples plus 15 bananas is higher, but one cannot say how much higher. An indifference curve which is determined in this way does not have to be based on interval scale properties but only needs to possess ordinal properties (Edwards 1954).

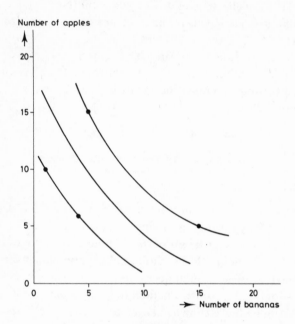

Fig. 2. Examples of indifference curves.

A totally different kind of criticism against the classical *homo economicus* model has been given by the organizational scientist H. A. Simon. He does not criticise the utility function but doubts whether all information about alternatives and actions is available to the decision-maker and whether the decision-maker really looks for optimal solutions (Simon 1947). A discussion of these criticisms falls outside the scope of this book.

1.3. Fuzzy States and Fuzzy Utilities

Suppose the decision situation can be characterized by a set of system states:

$$X = \{x_1, \ldots, x_n\},$$

a set of possible actions:

$$A = \{a_1, \ldots, a_m\},$$

and a utility matrix, $U = \{u_{ij}\}$, which assigns the utility of choosing alternative action a_i when the state of this system is x_j. Note that this is a slightly different formulation from that in the previous section. U is the utility function on $A \times X$ and is given by an $m \times n$ matrix:

$$U = \begin{bmatrix} u_{11} \text{----} u_{in} \\ \\ u_{mi} \text{---} u_{mn} \end{bmatrix}$$

The decision problem is simply that of finding the alternative action $a_i \in A$ which gives the highest utility for the given state x_j of the system: choose a_{io} such that:

$$u_{ioj} = \max_i u_{ij}.$$

Suppose that the states of the system are not known exactly, but that the knowledge about the state of the system is fuzzy (Jain 1976); then the state is a fuzzy set X with membership function:

$$\mu_X(x_j) \hspace{9cm} x_j \in X.$$

This fuzziness implies that the utility associated with each alternative $a_i \in A$ can no longer remain exact and that it becomes fuzzy. This fuzzy utility is a fuzzy set U_i with membership function:

$$\mu_{U_i}(u_{ij}) = \mu_x(x_j).$$

Not only the state of the system but also the utility itself may be fuzzy, so that the original utility matrix becomes a matrix of fuzzy sets $U = \{U_{ij}\}$ where each fuzzy utility is a fuzzy set U_{ij} with membership function:

$$\mu_{U_{ij}}(u_{ik}) \hspace{9cm} k = 1, \ldots n.$$

Suppose, for example, that $A = \{a_1, a_2, a_3\}$ and $X = \{x_1, \ldots x_{10}\}$

then the fuzzy utility U_{13} might be the fuzzy set 'low' defined by:

$$U_{13}(u_{11}) = 0.4$$
$$U_{13}(u_{12}) = 1.0$$
$$U_{13}(u_{13}) = 0.5$$

while all other membership values are zero.

In Jain (1976) a procedure is outlined on how to obtain the fuzzy set of optimal alternatives and on how to deduce the final optimal alternative action from that fuzzy set. We will now proceed with the combination of fuzziness and probabilistic decision-making. Although the probabilistic decision-making model has already been presented in the previous section we prefer to begin this fuzzy probabilistic part with a presentation of that same model in terms of probability theory, the well-known statistical decision theory, in order to show what is exactly meant by decision-making under risk and decision-making under uncertainty. For an extensive treatment of statistical decision theory see e.g. Wald (1950), Lehman (1959), Ferguson (1967).

1.4. Statistical decision theory

Mathematically viewed, decision-making is a mapping from the measurement space X to the decision space D. This mapping $\delta: X \to D$ is called the decision function: the elements $d \in D$ are called decisions. In order to determine a preference for a certain decision above other decisions, we introduce a loss function. This loss function depends on the decision $d \in D$ and on the probability distribution F_ϑ on the measurement space X, where ϑ parametrises the class of distributions:

$$F_\vartheta(x) = P_\vartheta(X < x).$$

The loss function thus becomes $L(\vartheta, d)$, $\vartheta \in \Theta, d \in D$.
The expected value of the loss will be:

$$E\{L(\vartheta, d)\} = E\{L(\vartheta, \delta(x))\} = R(\vartheta, \delta)$$

which is called the risk function.
We call d_1 uniformly better than d_2 where $d_1 = \delta_1(x)$ and $d_2 = \delta_2(x)$, if:

$$R(\vartheta, \delta_1) \leq R(\vartheta, \delta_2) \qquad \text{for all } \vartheta.$$
$$R(\vartheta, \delta_1) < R(\vartheta, \delta_2) \qquad \text{for at least one } \vartheta.$$

A class D of decisions is called complete if for every $d \notin D$, there exists a $d' \in D$ such that d' is uniformly better than d.

The minimising of $R(\vartheta, \delta)$ will also depend on the parameter ϑ which determines the distribution $F_\vartheta(x)$. In general it will not always be possible to find a $\delta(x)$ which minimises $R(\vartheta, \delta)$ for all possible ϑ. Now introduce a distribution $\varrho(\vartheta)$ for this parameter. The expected value of the risk of a decision function δ becomes

$$r(\varrho, \delta) = \int E_\vartheta \{L(\vartheta, \delta)\} \varrho(\vartheta) \, d\vartheta = \int R(\vartheta, \delta) \varrho(\vartheta) \, d\vartheta$$

and by definition, the smaller $r(\varrho, \delta)$, the better δ.
By definition the optimal δ' is given by

$$r(\varrho, \delta') = \inf_\delta r(\varrho, \delta).$$

This δ' is called a Bayes solution to the decision problem. This is the model of decision-making under risk. The model of decision-making under uncertainty follows.

If the prior information about the distribution $\varrho(\vartheta)$ is missing, we take the risk with the least favourable prior distribution, that is we consider the supremum over ϑ of the risk function $r(\vartheta, \delta)$. That decision function is chosen which minimises this $\sup_\vartheta r(\vartheta, \delta)$:

$$\inf_\delta \sup_\vartheta r(\vartheta, \delta).$$

This is called a minimax procedure. It is possible to prove that under not too strict conditions
- all Bayes solutions form a complete class;
- minimax procedures are Bayes solutions according to the least favourable prior distribution.

1.5. Fuzzy statistical decision theory

The extension of the statistical decision theory to a fuzzy statistical decision theory leads via the notion of a fuzzy event and the probability of a fuzzy event (Zadeh 1968). Let X and Y be sets of events $\{x_1 \ldots x_n\}$ and $\{y_1 \ldots y_m\}$ with probabilities $p(x_i)$ and $p(y_i)$ respectively. Fuzzy events A and B are fuzzy sets on X and Y characterised by their membership functions

$\mu_A : X \to [0,1]$ and $\mu_B : Y \to [0,1]$. Let $p(x_i, y_j)$ be the joint probability of x_i and y_j. The probability of a fuzzy event A is defined by:

$$P(A) = \sum_{i=1}^{n} \mu_A(x_i) \, p(x_i),$$

the joint probability of two fuzzy events A and B by

$$P(A, B) = \sum_i \sum_j \mu_A(x_i) \, \mu_B(y_j) \, p(x_i, y_j),$$

and the conditional probability of event A depending on B by

$$P(A/B) = P(A, B)/P(B) \qquad\qquad \text{where} \, p(B) > 0$$

with $P(A/y_j) = P(A, y_j)/p(y_j)$ $\qquad\qquad$ where $p(y_j) > 0$.

The factual extension of the probabilistic decision problem into a fuzzy probabilistic one is completed by everywhere replacing events with fuzzy events (Tanaka et al., 1976). The decision problem with fuzzy events is defined as a quadruple:

$$\langle X, A, p, u \rangle$$

where $X = \{X_1 \ldots X_r\}$ is a set of fuzzy states which are fuzzy events on a probabilistic space $\{x_i \ldots x_n\}$ as defined earlier. $A = \{A_1 \ldots A_q\}$ is a set of fuzzy actions which are fuzzy events on the action space $\{a_1 \ldots a_m\}$ and U is a utility function on $A \times X$.

The expected utility of a fuzzy action A_i is defined by:

$$U(A_i) = \sum_j U(A_i, X_j) P(X_j).$$

An optimal decision is defined as that fuzzy action which maximises $U(A_i)$:

$$U(A_0) = \max_i U(A_i).$$

Tanaka et al. (1976) extend this framework with a message space. Definitions are presented which deal with the value of information. Two kinds of information are considered: namely, information which contains exact knowledge about a true state x_i, this being called probabilistic perfect information, and information that tells which fuzzy state X_i occurs with probability one, this being called fuzzy perfect information.

This framework is applied to a project selection problem. The problem is defined as follows: assume that a succesful firm is in a position to expand its operations. Three courses of action are possible:

1. choose the small-scale project,
2. choose the middle-scale project, or
3. choose the large-scale project.

'Small', 'middle', and 'large' are defined as fuzzy sets. The utility of each investment depends on the national economy, which is duly simplified to correspond with economic growth. The messages consist of information about the rate of increase of national gross investments in the near-term future. One of the conclusions of their decision problem evaluation is that probabilistic perfect information is not so valuable as fuzzy perfect information.

1.6. Fuzzy random variables

A rather different approach to the fuzzy probabilistic decision problem is adopted by Van Eeden (1976). Starting from the definition of a fuzzy number as a fuzzy set defined on the real line R, the following definition of a fuzzy random variable is given:

a discrete fuzzy random variable $\underline{X}$ is defined as a set of pairs $\{(p_i, X_i), i = 1, 2 \ldots n\}$. Here p_i denotes the probability that the fuzzy number X_i occurs. For each $i : p_i \geqq 0, \Sigma p_i = 1$, while X_i is a membership function.

Note that here p_i is the probability that a fuzzy number occurs which corresponds to the above-mentioned probability of a fuzzy event.

The interpretation of a discrete fuzzy random variable is as follows. The total population underlying the probabilistic model is divided into n groups. The i-th group is a fraction p_i of the total population with an opinion represented by the fuzzy number X_i. The diversity of opinions within the i-th group is represented by the distribution function $F_i(x)$, $x \in R$.

According to the membership function $X_i(x)$, the degree of acceptability that the opinion is thus distributed is:

$$\inf_{x \,:\, F_i\,(dx)\,>\,0} X_i(x)$$

This leads to the following derivation of the expectation of a fuzzy random variable. The average opinion within the i-th group is

$$\int_{-\infty}^{\infty} x\,dF_i(x)$$

with a grade of membership.

$$\inf_{x \,:\, F_i\,(dx)\,>\,0} X_i\,(x).$$

The average opinion over all the groups, denoted by $\bar{x}$, is thus:

$$\bar{x} = \sum_{i=1}^{n} p_i \int_{-\infty}^{\infty} x\,dF_i(x)$$

with a grade of membership:

$$\min_{i} \quad \inf_{x \,:\, F_i\,(dx)\,>\,0} X_i\,(x).$$

Here the choice of the distribution functions F_i is still open. The expectation of the fuzzy random variable $\underline{X}$, denoted by $E\underline{X}$, is defined as a fuzzy number with membership function

$$(E\underline{X})\,(\bar{x}) = \sup\{\min_{i} \quad \inf_{x \,:\, F_i\,(dx)\,>\,0} X_i(x)\,|\,F_i(\,.\,), i = 1, 2, \ldots, n : \bar{x} =$$

$$\sum_{i=1}^{n} p_i \int_{-\infty}^{\infty} x\,dF_i(x)\}.$$

A similar approach is adopted for the definition of the conditional probability of a fuzzy random variable. In Van Eeden (1976) algorithms are proposed for the computation of these rather awkward formulas.

The theory of fuzzy random variables which has been presented is applied to a decision situation where a man wants to do his shopping in three stores: a bakery, a drug store, and a grocer's. The drug store is five minutes' walk from the man's office in one direction, while in the opposite direction the grocer's is two minutes' walk and the baker's four (Figure 3).

Fig. 3. Situation sketch.

The numbers of people waiting in the shops are characterised by the fuzzy numbers 'crowded', 'not crowded', and 'no recollection'. Serving times in the three shops are represented by the fuzzy numbers 'short', 'very short', and 'quite long' (figure 4).

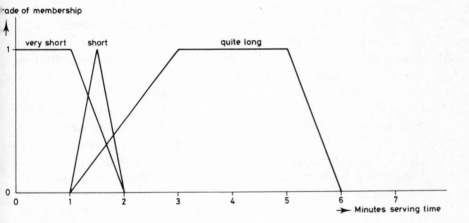

Fig. 4. Some fuzzy numbers.

Joint probabilities of the numbers of people waiting in the several shops are also given, plus some other detailed information.

The conclusions from the evaluation of this example are that the strict application of the theory does not permit one optimal solution to be chosen, although a preference for one of the alternatives was found. The characterisation and interpretation of calculated membership functions may have a great effect on conclusions from calculations with fuzzy random variables (Van Eeden 1976).

1.7. Discussion

The extension of the classical model of individual decision-making – maximisation of (expected) utility – into a fuzzy version is straightforward and simple. Likewise is the extension of statistical decision theory into fuzzy statistical decision theory. It is not clear which short-comings or problems within these theories led to this extension – in other words, which particular kinds of problems or which practical situations arose in this classical theory where fuzziness could offer relief. Apart from the general rationale that fuzziness enters almost every decision situation, no such reasons are given. Practical examples would lead us to think that situations where the variables can no longer be expressed numerically but only in linguistic terms are typical problem situations for fuzzy statistical decision theory. However, the use of linguistic variables (see also Section 7.2) does not imply that probabilistic methods should be employed. Almost every fuzzy theory makes use of linguistic variables when it comes to practical examples.

Without these specific reasons the extension into fuzzy statistical decision theory looks rather like one of so many fuzzifications of conventional theories. This also implies that several problems within statistical decision theory, in particular problems concerning the application of the theory, are in fact overlooked – e.g. the problem of the determination of the utility function (Luce and Raiffa 1957, Fishburn 1964 and 1970). In practical situations the underlying requirements of the utility functions are often not met. One might hope that a theory which purports to be especially applicable to real-world problems can at least solve some existing ones first.

Another problem which has been raised but not at all settled as yet is the relationship between fuzziness and probability. Many authors have stressed the differences between the concepts and actually it seems easy to explain the difference between a frequentistic view of probability and the fuzzy concept of vagueness. Things grow more difficult when we compare fuzziness with subjective probability. It becomes still more difficult when both concepts are mixed together.

A recent brief survey of literature concerning the relationship between fuzzy sets and probability theory (Gaines and Kohout 1977: section 2.7) shows that little specific research into this relationship has yet been performed. Research into the logical foundations of both concepts has shown some essential differences (Gaines 1976a, b). On the other hand critics of the fuzzy approach who argue that fuzziness and subjectivity are dealt with equally by the adoption of a Bayes approach on the basis of subjective probabilities, are not convinced by a long way (see e.g. Stallings 1977). Although every fuzzy researcher seems to have an intuitive notion of the distinctions between fuzziness and probability and it is actually clear that there definitely are some fundamental differences between (subjective) probability and fuzziness, it is strange that so little work has been done on this subject. A theory of what the differences are and particularly a translation of such a theory into operational terms of where to use what concept and what for is urgently needed. Apart from the fundamental investigations in (Gaines 1976a, b) and the sporadic studies where the practical differences are studied by applying the two concepts and comparing them – such as the comparison of a fuzzy approach and a probabilistic approach to multicriteria analysis in Baas and Kwakernaak (1975, see also section 4.4), the reanalysis of the fuzzy logic control strategy of Mamdani and Assilian (1975) by Gaines (1975) using a probability logic, and the reanalysis of the fuzzy pattern recognition algorithm of Kickert and Koppelaar (1976) by Stallings (1977) using a probabilistic Bayes approach – such a theory is still missing.

2. Fuzzy decision-making under constraints

2.1. Introduction

The particular kind of fuzzy decision-making which will be presented in this chapter describes the decision situation viewed as an optimisation under constraints. The situation is here defined as follows. Given:

– a set of decision variables;
– a set of constraints on these decision variables; and
– an objective function which orders the alternatives according to their desirability,

find the (optimal) solution.

This is clearly the operation research type of decision problem formulation – mathematical programming – which is best known mainly because of the famous linear programming technique that has been shown to be of great practical use.

It is not hard to imagine situations where a deterministic or even a probabilistic approach does not apply. When the decision-maker is no longer able to specify exactly his constraints and his objective, either because that is just impossible or because he wants to allow himself some leeway, and these quantities can only be stated in such terms as 'much bigger', 'near to', etc., neither the notion of determinism nor of probability is satisfactory. In this chapter it will be shown that in these situations the theory of fuzzy sets might be helpful.

2.2. Decision-making in a fuzzy environment

Before treating the theory itself it seems useful to look somewhat closer at the particular kind of fuzzy decision situation comprised by that theory. As stated before, the situation splits up into the following points: the decision variables, the constraints, and the goals. The notion of fuzziness might be introduced into all these basic elements. The theory of fuzzy mathematical programming restricts itself to fuzziness at only one level, namely that of constraints and goals. The decision variables are considered to remain deterministic (or at most probabilistic). Only the goals and constraints constitute classes of alternatives whose boundaries are not sharply defined.

Having tried to clarify the general setting and boundaries of the theory, let us now pass to the theory itself (Bellman and Zadeh 1970). The fuzzy objective function, as well as the fuzzy constraint, are characterised by their membership function. The aim is to satisfy both the goals and the constraints; hence a fuzzy decision is considered to be the intersection of the fuzzy constraints and the fuzzy goals. An important feature of the theory is the symmetry between goals and constraints. Both are essentially similar concepts, which makes it possible to relate easily the concept of a fuzzy decision to those of the goals and constraints.

Let us now define the general framework of the fuzzy mathematical programming theory:

Let X be a set of possible alternative decision actions. A fuzzy goal G is a fuzzy subset on X characterized by its membership function $\mu_G : X \to [0, 1]$. A fuzzy constraint C is a fuzzy subset on X, characterised by its membership function $\mu_C : X \to [0, 1]$.

The fuzzy decision D resulting from the fuzzy goal G and the fuzzy constraint C is the intersection of both, so:

$$D = G \cap C$$

and is characterised by its membership function

$$\mu_D(x) = \min[\mu_G(x); \mu_C(x)] \qquad\qquad x \in X$$

More generally the decision D resulting from n fuzzy goals $G_1 \ldots G_n$ and m fuzzy constraints $C_1 \ldots C_m$ is defined by:

$$\mu_D = \left(\bigwedge_{i=1}^{n} \mu_{Gi} \right) \wedge \left(\bigwedge_{j=1}^{m} \mu_{Cj} \right).$$

For example, suppose that we have a goal G and a constraint C expressed as:

G : x should be much larger than 5.
C : x should be near 10 (Figure 5).

where:

$$\mu_G(x) = 1 - (1 + (0.2(x-5))^2)^{-1} \quad \text{for } x > 5, \text{ elsewhere } \mu_{G(x)} = 0$$

and

$$\mu_C(x) = (1 + (x-10)^2)^{-1}.$$

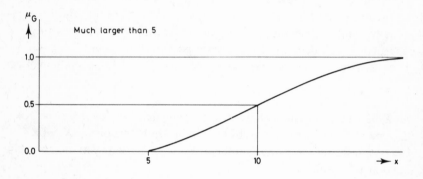

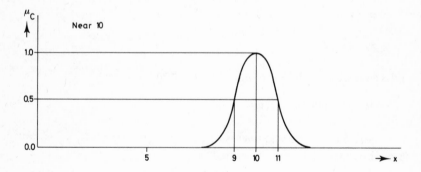

Fig. 5. Fuzzy goal and fuzzy constraint.

The fuzzy decision D is the intersection of both fuzzy sets,

$$D = G \cap C.$$

and is illustrated in Figure 6.

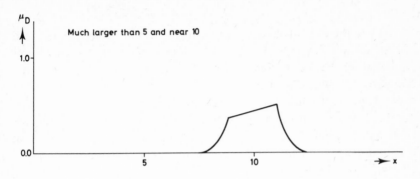

Figure 6. Fuzzy decision.

Goals and constraints

In the conventional approach the direction in which the decision process should develop is mostly induced by an objective or performance function, which in conventional decision theory is usually called the utility function. This function ranks the set of alternatives according to the preference of the decision-maker. Although there is no mention of an objective function but of a (fuzzy) goal, it is clear that the membership function, $\mu_G(x)$, serves the same purpose (with the condition that the membership function takes values in an ordered set). The concept of 'degree of membership of x in the goal G' is not far away from the concept of 'level of acceptance of x in view of the goal G' which corresponds to a preference ordering of the alternative decision actions $x \in X$. The reason for adopting this slightly different notion lies in the fact that goals and constraints can now be treated in the same way, both being mathematically identical concepts, whereas in conventional mathematical programming goals and constraints are treated differently.

Because a decision is considered to satisfy goals and constraints, its definition as the intersection of these two seems self-evident. It should, however, be noted that the usual definition of intersection as the minimum operation is arbitrary and has the disadvantage of a lack of interdependence. In other words, as long as $\mu_A \geq \mu_B$, the intersection $\mu_A \wedge \mu_B$ is absolutely independent of the value of μ_A. If one whishes the fuzzy decision to reflect always the values of the constituent goals and constraints, one might introduce an alternative definition such as:

$$\mu_D(x) = \left(\prod_{i=1}^{n} \mu_{G_i}(x) \right) \cdot \left(\prod_{j=1}^{m} \mu_{C_j}(x) \right).$$

Essentially the sort of definition of a fuzzy decision comes down to the desired semantic meaning and hence definition of the intersection ('and'). Note that the definition of the intersection is closely coupled to that of the union ('or') in the sense that one wants both operations to possess at least some algebraic elegance (associativity, distributivity, etc).

The problem of the semantics of the fuzzy connective 'and' has been investigated rather extensively, both empirically (Rödder 1975) and theoretically (Hamacher 1975). For a treatment of this problem see the epilogue to this book.

Evaluation of the fuzzy decision

The next addition which has to be made concerns the evaluation of the fuzzy decision. Although there may be situations where the decision-maker is satisfied with solutions in the form of fuzzy sets – for example, 'x is much greater than 7' and 'x approximately between 10 and 12' – it is understandable that many situations occur where the final decision to be made has to be exact, well-defined, hence non-fuzzy. In other words, how should the resulting fuzzy decision be evaluated to obtain a representative non-fuzzy decision.

One way to evaluate a fuzzy decision D is by splitting the fuzzy set into its α-level sets. An α-level set (or α-cut) R_α of a fuzzy set D on X is defined by

$$R_\alpha = \{x \in X \mid \mu_D(x) \geq \alpha\}.$$

This α-level set is obviously a non-fuzzy set. By means of this concept one can construct a series of sets according to their truth (agreement, or confidence) levels. This might give some insight into the fuzzy decision but does not yet lead to one particular single decision.

A very easy way is to look for that decision where the fuzzy decision attains its maximum membership function. Let us define the optimal (or maximum) decision set M of the fuzzy goal G by:

$$M = \{x_0 \in X \mid \mu_G(x_0) = \sup_{x \in X} \mu_G(x)\}.$$

Notice that additional restrictions should be imposed on G to ensure that there is only one $x_0 \in M$. Mostly M consists of more than one element.

A very simple final evaluation might consist of taking the mean x_M of all $x_0 \in M$ and to let x_M represent the fuzzy set G. This evaluation procedure is arbitrary and has the disadvantage that it depends only on the maxima of the fuzzy set. The rest of the fuzzy set – its form or shape – is not considered at all. An evaluation procedure to map the fuzzy set G in one single representative value x_G, which takes into account the shape of G, might be to take:

$$x_G = \int_X \mu_G(x) \cdot x\, dx / \int_X \mu_G(x)\, dx$$

which is essentially the centre of gravity of a fuzzy set. This latter procedure has the disadvantage of introducing the algebraic product and sum (integral) operators into a framework where minimum and maximum operators prevail. Cross-combinations of these operators lack some useful algebraic properties such as distributivity and associativity.

A different approach to the evaluation problem may be that, instead of deriving a single, exact, non-fuzzy decision value from a fuzzy decision, one should assign a linguistic value to that fuzzy decision.

Given a set of basic linguistic values like 'big', 'small', etc., a set of linguistic hedges like 'very', 'rather', 'more or less', the set of usual connectives 'and', 'or', 'not', one may construct an evaluation procedure which assigns to the resulting fuzzy decision a linguistic term such as, for example, 'not small and not very big'. This term should be a well-formed formula, which means that the term should be composed of the basic linguistic values, the hedges, and the connectives, according to the rules of a generative grammar. This grammar generates the allowed linguistic terms. Iteratively the generated term is compared with the actual fuzzy decision, and according to some best-fitting criterion, the term is either assigned to the decision or not (Wenstøp 1976). Kaufmann (1975b: section 89) presents some other appealing criteria for the assignment of linguistic terms to fuzzy decisions (Figure 7).

The theory of linguistic variables and the assignment of linguistic terms to fuzzy outputs will be treated in greater detail in Section 7.2.

Different support sets

A last extension which is discussed in this sub-section is the case where goals and constraints are no longer defined on the same support set of alternative decision actions X. A more general case which is surely of practical interest

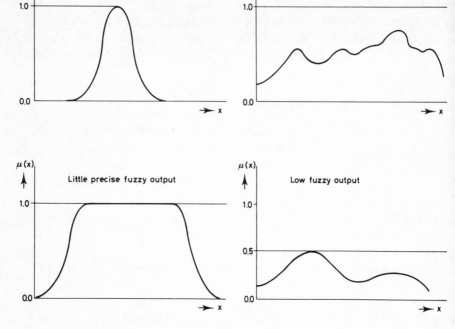

Fig. 7. Assignment of linguistic terms to fuzzy decisions.

is the case where two sets exist, namely a set of causes X and a set of effects Y, where both sets are related via a function: $f : X \rightarrow Y$. Now suppose that the fuzzy goals are defined as fuzzy sets $G_1 \ . \ . \ . \ G_n$ on Y, whereas the fuzzy constraints $C_1 \ . \ . \ . \ C_m$ are defined as fuzzy sets on X. Construct the fuzzy sets G_i in X which induce the fuzzy goals G_i on Y by taking:

$$\mu_{G_i}(x) = \mu_{G_i}(f(x)) = \mu_{G_i}(y), \qquad\qquad\qquad y = f(x).$$

The decision D can still be expressed as an intersection of goals and constraints on X, namely by:

$$\mu_D(x) = \left[\bigwedge_{i=1}^{n} \mu_{G_i}(f(x)) \right] \wedge \left[\bigwedge_{j=1}^{m} \mu_{C_j}(x) \right]$$

where $f : X \rightarrow Y$. This notion will return in the analysis of multi-stage decision processes.

2.3. Fuzzy and non-fuzzy mathematical programming

We will discuss the relationship between fuzzy mathematical programming and conventional mathematical programming first on a general level and later on a more practical level (Section 2.4).

Assume an objective function $f : X \to R^+$ where X is the set of alternatives. Take $X = R^n$. Also assume a fuzzy constraint C on X characterized by its membership function $\mu_C : X \to [0, 1]$. Now suppose that f is bounded: $f(x) \leqq M, x \in X$. Then by taking $\mu_G(x) = f(x)/M$ so that μ_G is indeed a function taking values between 0 and 1, $\mu_G : X \to [0, 1]$, we have now transformed the objective function into a fuzzy goal. The fuzzy mathematical programming problem consists of finding the maximum of the fuzzy decision D:

$$\sup_{x \in X} \mu_D(x) = \sup_{x \in X} [\mu_C(x) \wedge \mu_G(x)].$$

In Tanaka et al. (1974), and Negoita and Ralescu (1975: section 6-1), a theorem is presented which shows that, with some assumptions, this problem reduces to the conventional mathematical programming problem of finding the maximum:

$$\sup_{x \in A} \mu_G(x)$$

subject to the constraint:

$$A = \{x \in X \,|\, \mu_C(x) - \mu_G(x) \geq 0\}.$$

More generally this theorem also holds in case of n fuzzy constraints $C_1 \ldots C_n$ on X, in which case one simply takes

$$C = C_1 \cap C_2 \cap \ldots \cap C_n.$$

The proof of this theorem will not be given here. Only the essential steps in the proof will be outlined. First it is proved that:

$$\sup_{x \in X} \mu_D(x) = \sup_{\alpha \in [0, 1]} [\alpha \wedge \sup_{x \in C_\alpha} \mu_G(x)]$$

where $C_\alpha = \{x \in X \,|\, \mu_C(x) \geq \alpha\}$ is the α-level set of C. This also holds when $C = C_1 \cap \ldots \cap C_n$. Then it is proved that a solution to the problem exists:

Define $\varphi(\alpha) = \sup\limits_{x \in C_\alpha} \mu_G(x)$.

If φ is continuous on $[0, 1]$ then

$$\exists \alpha \in [0, 1] \text{ so that } \varphi(\bar{\alpha}) = \bar{\alpha}$$

and $\quad \sup\limits_{x \in X} \mu_D(x) = \bar{\alpha} = \varphi(\bar{\alpha})$

Finally it is proved that $C_{\bar{\alpha}} \subset A$ so that:

$$\sup\limits_{x \in A} \mu_G(x) \geq \sup\limits_{x \in C_{\bar{\alpha}}} \mu_G(x) = \bar{\alpha}$$

and hence

$$\sup\limits_{x \in X} \mu_D(x) = \sup\limits_{x \in A} \mu_G(x)$$

which ends the proof of the original theorem.

The assumption that $\varphi(\alpha)$ is continuous on $\alpha = [0, 1]$ is sufficiently satisfied by the condition that $\mu_C(x)$ must be strictly convex. By definition a fuzzy subset: $R^n \rightarrow [0, 1]$ is called strictly convex if for all x, y out of the support set of μ, $x \neq y$

$$\mu(\lambda x + (1 - \lambda) y) > \mu(x) \wedge \mu(y)$$

for all $\lambda \in [0, 1]$.

So far we have discussed the relationship between mathematical programming and fuzzy mathematical programming on a general level. We will now proceed with the comparison of the fuzzy and non-fuzzy linear programming methods.

2.4. Fuzzy and non-fuzzy linear programming

Apart from the general proof of the identity between a certain fuzzy mathematical programming problem and a conventional mathematical programming (MP) problem, one may try to find similarities and analogies at a practical level. The most obvious practical field of MP is that of linear programming (LP), and it is not surprising that extensions into fuzzy LP have attracted the interest of researchers.

The first such extension was undertaken by Zimmermann (1976). He fuzzifies the usual linear programming problem: minimise $Z = cx$, subject to the constraints $Ax \leq b$ and $x \geq 0$, into the fuzzy version:

$$cx \lessgtr Z$$
$$Ax \lessgtr b$$
$$x \gtreqless 0$$

where c is the vector of coefficients of the objective function, b is the vector of constraints, and A is the coefficient matrix. The symbol $\lessgtr$ denotes 'essentially smaller than or equal to'. This fuzzy inequality concept is operationalised by taking as its membership function a function f which should at least satisfy the following external conditions:

$$f(Ax, cx) = \begin{cases} 0 \text{ if } Ax \leq b \text{ and } cx \leq Z \text{ is strongly violated} \\ 1 \text{ if } Ax \geq b \text{ and } cx \geq Z \text{ is satisfied} \end{cases}$$

and which between these extremes indicates the level of violation or acceptability of the combinations of variables Ax and cx. The simplest version of such a function is a linear one which gradually increases from zero to one between the extremes.

Moreover, if we consider the constraints $Ax \lessgtr b$ and the goals $cx \lessgtr Z$ to be two mathematically identical concepts – as is the aim of the definition of a fuzzy decision – and define the decision as the intersection of both, we arrive at the following membership function for the fuzzy inequality concept:

$$f(Bx) = \min_i f_i((Bx)_i)$$

with

$$f_i((Bx)_i) = \begin{cases} 1 & \text{for } (Bx)_i \leq b_i \\ 1 - \dfrac{(Bx)_i - b_i}{d_i} & \text{for } b_i < (Bx)_i \leq b_i + d_i \\ 0 & \text{for } (Bx)_i > b_i + d_i \end{cases}$$

where B is a matrix formed by adding the row c to the matrix A, and where $f_i((Bx)_i)$ is the function of the i-th row $(Bx)_i$ of the system Bx.

The interpretation of the d_i is that these are constants of admissible violations of the constraints. The final function

$$\min_i f_i((Bx)_i)$$

is the 'fuzzy decision' of the problem, which corresponds to the usual definition of that concept as the intersection of fuzzy goals and constraints. The problem of finding the maximum decision:

$$\max_x \min_i f_i((Bx)_i)$$

can be shown to be equivalent to the linear programming problem. Substitute

$$b'_i = \frac{b_i}{d_i}$$

$$B'_i = \frac{B_i}{d_i}$$

and drop the 1 from the $f_i((Bx)_i)$ function. This given the following reduction of the problem:

$$\max_{x \geq 0} \min_i (b'_i - (Bx)_i).$$

This problem is equivalent to the solution of the conventional linear programming problem:

maximise λ
subject to constraints $\lambda \leq b_i - (Bx)_i$
$$x \geq 0.$$

In Negoita and Sularia (1976) the identity which Zimmermann noted for linear membership functions is proved to hold in general.

Given a set of alternatives X, a set of m fuzzy constraints $f_i : X \rightarrow [0, 1]$,

$i = 1, \ldots m$, and a fuzzy goal $f_0 : X \rightarrow [0, 1]$, the fuzzy decision problem is to find $x^* \in X$ such that:

$$\mu_D(x^*) = \sup_x \mu_D(x) = \sup_x \min_{i=0,1,\ldots m} f_i(x)$$

The alternative $x^* \in X$ is an optimal decision if the vector $(x^*, \lambda) \in R \times [0, 1]$ where $\lambda = \min_{i=0,\ldots m} f_i(x^*)$ is a solution of the linear programme:

find max λ
subject to $\lambda < f_i(x)$ $i = 1, \ldots, m, x \in R$
$\lambda \geq 0$

Applications

In Zimmermann (1976) the method is applied to a decision on the size and structure of a truck fleet. In this case both the non-fuzzy conventional and the fuzzy method are applied and compared.

Four differently sized trucks (x_1 to x_4) were considered. The objective was to minimise costs, and the constraints were that certain minimum quantities had to be transported and that a minimum number of customers had to be visited each day. In addition, at least six of the smallest trucks had to be included in the fleet.

The suggested linear programming approach was: minimise

$$41,000x_1 + 44,300x_2 + 48,100x_3 + 49,100x_4$$

subject to the constraints:

$$0.84x_1 + 1.44x_2 + 2.16x_3 + 2.40x_4 \geq 170$$
$$16x_1 + 16x_2 + 16x_3 + 16x_4 \geq 1300$$
$$x_1 \geq 6.$$

The solution was $x_1 = 6$, $x_2 = 17.85$, $x_3 = 0$, $x_4 = 58.64$ with costs $= 3,918,850$. The flexible formulation of the problem in the form of a fuzzy linear programme is shown in table 2.

Table 2: Fuzzy problem formulation.

Non-fuzzy		Fuzzy $\mu = 0$	$\mu = 1$
Objective function		4,200,000	3,700,000
First constraint	170	170	180
Second constraint	1,300	1,300	1,400
Third constraint	6	6	12

The equivalent non-fuzzy problem is then: maximise λ, subject to the constraints:

$$\lambda \leq 7.4 - 0.083x_1 - 0.089x_2 - 0.096x_3 - 0.098x_4$$
$$\lambda \leq -18 + 0.084x_1 + 0.144x_2 + 0.216x_3 + 0.24x_4$$
$$\lambda \leq -14 + 0.16x_1 + 0.16x_2 + 0.16x_3 + 0.16x_4$$
$$\lambda \leq -2 + 0.167$$
$$x_1, x_2, x_3, x_4 \geq 0$$

which gives a solution as set out in table 3.

Table 3: Solutions of both linear programmes.

Non-fuzzy	Fuzzy
$x_1 = 6$	$x_1 = 17.41$
$x_2 = 17.85$	$x_4 = 66.54$
$x_4 = 58.65$	
$Z = 3,918,850$	$Z = 3,988,257$
Constraints	
1. 171.5	174.2
2. 1,320	1,342.4
3. 6	17.4

The decision-maker was no longer forced to formulate the problem in a mathematically rigorous way merely because of the requirements of the method. He is only able or willing to give vague problem formulation in terms of upper and lower limits and is therefore faced with additional costs of some 1.7%.

In Rödder and Zimmermann (1977) the same approach is applied to the design of a parking place. Essentially the approach consists of a straightforward fuzzification of the objective and constraints of a linear programming problem, resulting in the equivalent fuzzy goals and constraints from which the fuzzy decision is derived in the usual way. The particular choice of the membership function reflects the major advantage of the method: constraints do not have to be precise numbers but are defined as boundary ranges.

2.5. Fuzzy linear programming and tolerance analysis

In Negoita et al. (1976) the fuzzy linear programming (FLP) problem is tackled by first reducing the FLP problem to a LP problem with set coefficients, which in its turn can be transformed into a conventional LP problem. The fuzzy linear problem that they consider has the following formulation:

$$\sup c \cdot x$$
$$x_1 \underset{\sim}{K}_1 + x_2 \underset{\sim}{K}_2 + \ldots + x_n \underset{\sim}{K}_n \subset \underset{\sim}{K}$$
$$x_j \geq 0 \qquad j = 1, \ldots n$$

where c is a vector of coefficients, while $\underset{\sim}{K}_1$ to $\underset{\sim}{K}_n$ and $\underset{\sim}{K}$ are fuzzy sets. This problem is reduced to a LP problem with set coefficients by using the concept of a level set. Let A be a fuzzy set with $\mu_A(x)$. Then the α-level set (or cut-set) of A is defined as:

$$R_\alpha(A) = \{x \in X \mid \mu_A(x) \geq \alpha\}.$$

Note that this is a conventional set.
Level sets have, among others, the following properties:

$$\text{if } \alpha \leq \beta \text{ then } R_\beta(A) \subset R_\alpha(A)$$
$$A \subset B \text{ iff } R_\alpha(A) \subset R_\alpha(B) \qquad \forall \alpha \in [0, 1]$$

Moreover if we construct the fuzzy set $\alpha R_\alpha(A)$ defined by:

$$\mu_{\alpha R_\alpha}(x) = \alpha \text{ for } x \in R_\alpha(A)$$
$$0 \text{ elsewhere}$$

it can easily be proved that the fuzzy set can be composed of the level sets (see Appendix):

$$A = \bigcup_{\alpha \in [0,1]} \alpha R_\alpha(A).$$

Because of this last property the fuzzy LP problem can be reformulated as a set of LP problems of the form:

$$\sup c.x$$
$$x_1 R_\alpha(\underset{\sim}{K}_1) + x_2 R_\alpha(\underset{\sim}{K}_2) + \ldots + x_n R_\alpha(\underset{\sim}{K}_n) \subset R_\alpha(\underset{\sim}{K})$$
$$x_j \geqq 0 \quad \forall \alpha \in [0, 1].$$

If the fuzzy set $\underset{\sim}{K}$ has the property that its membership function assumes only a limited number of values:

$$\mu_{\underset{\sim}{K}} \in \{\alpha_1 \ldots \alpha_p\}$$
$$\text{with } 0 \leqq \alpha_1 < \alpha_2 \ldots < \alpha_p \leqq 1.$$

then the infinite set of problems reduces to the finite set of LP problems with set coefficients:

$$\sup c.x$$
$$x_1 R_{\alpha_i}(\underset{\sim}{K}_1) + x_2 R_{\alpha_i}(\underset{\sim}{K}_2) + \ldots + x_n R_{\alpha_i}(\underset{\sim}{K}_n) \subset R_{\alpha_i}(\underset{\sim}{K})$$
$$x_j \geqq 0, j = 1 \;, \ldots n \;, i = 1, \ldots p.$$

The next step consists of the reduction of a LP problem with set coefficients to an ordinary LP problem. Consider a set $\{K_1, K_2, \ldots, K_n\}$ of non-empty convex sets and another convex set K, all in R^m. We have the following problem:

$$\sup c.x$$
$$x_1 K_1 + x_2 K_2 + \ldots + x_n K_n \subset K$$
$$x_j \geqq 0, j = 1, \ldots n$$

which is termed a 'LP problem with set coefficients'. Assume, moreover, that K has the form

$$K = \{y \in R^m \,|\, y \leq b\}.$$

Thus formulated, the problem can be solved by constructing a vector a with components:

$$\overline{a}_j = \sup_{a_j \in K_j} a_j.$$

If the LP problem with set coefficients consists of a collection of such problems, we have to construct a matrix $\overline{A}$ with components

$$\overline{a}_{ij} = \sup_{a_j \in K_j} a_{ij}$$

where a_{ij} is the i-th row component of a_j.

Suppose that $\overline{a}_{ij} < \infty$. Now it can be proved that the admissible solutions of the conventional LP

$$\begin{aligned} \max \ c \ . \ x \\ \overline{A}x \leq b \\ x \geq 0 \end{aligned}$$

are also the admissible solutions of the LP problem with set coefficients. If K has the form

$$K = \{y \in R^m \,|\, y \geq b\}$$

then we have to replace a_{ij} by

$$\inf_{a_j \in K_j} a_{ij}$$

and the constraint in the LP is replaced by $\overline{A}x \geq b$.

In Negoita et al. (1976) the following example is given:

Consider a LP problem with set coefficients in the form of intervals:

$$[0.02 - 0.03] \, x_1 + [0.05 - 0.06] \, x_2 \subset [10.5 - 15.6]$$
$$[0.1 - 0.5] \, x_1 - [0.01 - 0.02] \, x_2 \subset [0.35 - 0.53]$$
minimise $3x_1 + 2x_2$
where $x_1 > x_2 \geq 0$.

This problem can be rewritten as:

$$0.03x_1 + 0.06x_2 \leq 15.6$$
$$0.05x_1 - 0.01x_2 \leq 0.53$$
$$0.02x_1 + 0.05x_2 \geq 10.5$$
$$0.01x_1 - 0.02x_2 \geq 0.35$$
$$x_1, x_2 \geq 0$$

minimise $3x_1 + 2x_2$.

Thus the original LP problem with fuzzy set coefficients can now be transformed via a LP problem with set coefficients into a conventional LP problem. Obviously disadvantage of the fuzzy LP problem lies in the dimensionality. However, conventional LP techniques are well-known and relatively easy to handle.

This may be illustrated by the example given in Negoita et al. (1976). Suppose that the problem is to find:

$$\max 2x_1 + 3x_2$$

subject to

$$\underset{\sim}{A}_{11}x_1 + \underset{\sim}{A}_{12}x_2 \subset \underset{\sim}{B}_1$$
$$\underset{\sim}{A}_{21}x_1 + \underset{\sim}{A}_{22}x_2 \subset \underset{\sim}{B}_2$$

with the fuzzy sets of Figure 8.

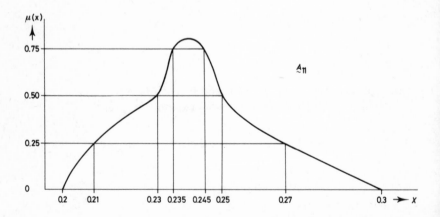

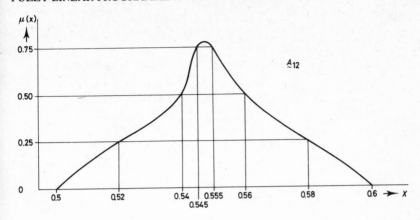

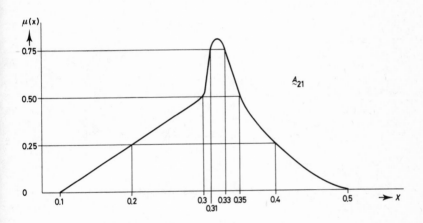

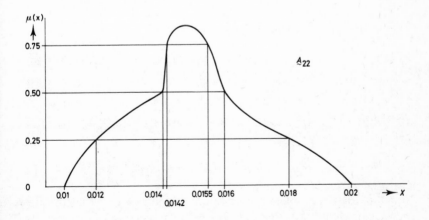

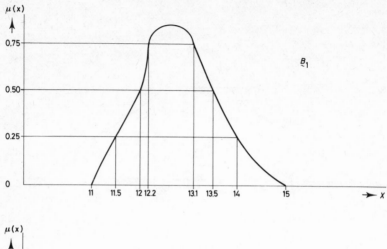

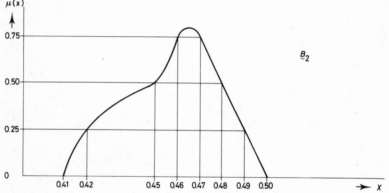

Fig. 8. The fuzzy set coefficients.

This gives the following level sets (intervals):

$A_0^{11} = [0.2., 0.3]$ $A_{0.25}^{11} = [0.21, 0.27]$ $A_{0.5}^{11} = [0.23, 0.25]$ $A_{0.75}^{11} = [0.235, 0.24]$

$A_0^{12} = [0.5, 0.6]$ $A_{0.25}^{12} = [0.52, 0.58]$ $A_{0.5}^{12} = [0.54, 0.56]$ $A_{0.75}^{12} = [0.545, 0.55]$

$A_0^{21} = [0.1, 0.5]$ $A_{0.25}^{21} = [0.2, 0.4]$ $A_{0.5}^{21} = [0.3, 0.35]$ $A_{0.75}^{21} = [0.31, 0.33]$

$A_0^{22} = [0.01, 0.02]$ $A_{0.25}^{22} = [0.012, 0.018]$ $A_{0.5}^{22} = [0.014, 0.016]$ $A_{0.75}^{22} = [0.0142, 0.0155]$

$B_0^{1} = [11, 15]$ $B_{0.25}^{1} = [11.5, 14]$ $B_{0.5}^{1} = [12, 13.5]$ $B_{0.75}^{1} = [12.2, 13.1]$

$B_0^{2} = [0.41, 0.5]$ $B_{0.25}^{2} = [0.42, 0.49]$ $B_{0.5}^{2} = [0.45, 0.48]$ $B_{0.75}^{2} = [0.46, 0.47]$

Now the original problem can be reformulated as a LP problem with set coefficients (intervals): find max $2x_1 + 3x_2$ subject to:

$$[0.2, 0.3] x_1 + \qquad [0.5, 0.6] x_2 \subset [11, 15]$$
$$[0.1, 0.5] x_1 + \qquad [0.01, 0.02] x_2 \subset [0.41, 0.5]$$
$$[0.21, 0.27] x_1 + \qquad [0.52, 0.58] x_2 \subset [11.5, 14]$$
$$[0.2, 0.4] x_1 + \quad [0.012, 0.018] x_2 \subset [0.42, 0.49]$$

. . . .

$$[0.31, 0.33] x_1 + [0.0142, 0.0155] x_2 \subset [0.46, 0.47]$$

Finally we reduce these problems to the conventional LP problem:

$$0.3 \ x_1 + 0.6 \ \ x_2 \leq 15 \qquad\qquad 0.25 \ x_1 + 0.56 \ \ x_2 \leq 13.5$$
$$0.2 \ x_1 + 0.5 \ \ x_2 \geq 11 \qquad\qquad 0.23 \ x_1 + 0.54 \ \ x_2 \geq 12$$
$$0.5 \ x_1 + 0.01 \ x_2 \leq 0.5 \qquad\qquad 0.35 \ x_1 + 0.014 \ x_2 \leq 0.45$$
$$0.1 \ x_1 + 0.02 \ x_2 \geq 0.41 \qquad\qquad 0.3 \ \ \ x_1 - 0.016 \ x_2 \geq 0.45$$
$$0.27 x_1 + 0.58 \ x_2 \leq 14 \qquad\qquad 0.245 x_1 + 0.555 \ x_2 \leq 13.1$$
$$0.21 x_1 + 0.52 \ x_2 \geq 11.5 \qquad\qquad 0.33 \ \ x_1 - 0.0142 x_2 \geq 0.47$$
$$0.4 \ x_1 + 0.012 x_1 \leq 0.49 \qquad\qquad 0.31 \ \ x_1 - 0.0155 x_2 \leq 0.46$$
$$0.2 \ x_1 + 0.018 x_2 \geq 0.42 \qquad\qquad 0.235 x_1 + 0.545 \ x_2 \geq 12.2$$

which can be easily solved by conventional LP techniques.

The advantage of incorporating imprecision, and thus flexibility, in this technique is paid for by enlarging the problem dimension. Note that this last form of fuzzy LP problem differs from that previously considered. Zimmermann (1976) formulates his fuzzy linear programme by fuzzifying the constraint inequalities, while in the last form Negoita et al. (1976) present their fuzzy linear programme as a LP problem with fuzzy set coefficients.

2.6. Discussion

Fuzzy mathematical programming has been shown to be of practical relevance. An important advantage of the method is that decision-makers are no longer compelled to state exactly the required constraints, something which is absolutely necessary when using conventional MP techniques. Admitting imprecision into the problem formulation might help greatly in situations where boundaries are not sharp but remain only boundary regions, and the incorporation of imprecise constraints makes the technique highly flexible.

The second great advantage of the method considered is that the fuzzy mathematical programme can be converted into a conventional MP problem, and can therefore be solved by means of conventional programming techniques. This last fact is obviously important because of the relatively large number of existing mathematical programming techniques and algorithms.

The formulation of a fuzzy LP problem as a LP problem with fuzzy set coefficients, as was considered second, also has both these advantages. However, it has the disadvantage of becoming a very large problem when transformed into conventional LP. It is not clear which advantage in this particular formulation of a fuzzy LP problem may compensate for this dimensional disadvantage.

It looks as if the flight taken by mathematical programming, and by linear programming in particular, will also be followed by fuzzy mathematical programming. On the one hand, this is not surprising at all in view of the real practical advantages that can be offered over conventional mathematical programming, which itself is already quite practical. On the other hand, it is a bit disappointing that fuzzy scientists prefer to remain at home in the safe Operations Research (OR) field rather than explore new fields. For it is well-known that LP (contrary to what some OR scientists might still believe) is not applicable to all decision problems. In my opinion this incrementalism – searching for solutions only in the neighbourhood of old solutions – does not guarantee great and quick discoveries.

3. Fuzzy multi-person decision-making

3.1. Introduction

n-person-making $(n \geq 2)$ is mostly considered in the framework of game theory as originated by Von Neumann and Morgenstern (1944). The decision process viewed as a game consists of a set of decision-makers, their possible alternative actions, the consequences thereof, and the utility values which are attached to those consequences (inducing a preference ordering). The essential difference between a decision made by one person and a decision made by more than one person can be divided into two aspects:

1. the preference ordering, or generally speaking the aims and values of each decision-maker can differ from those of the others.
2. the information upon which each decision-maker decides about his actions can differ from that of the others.

The available theories on n-person decision-making can now be grouped into three kinds, namely a theory which only deals with the first aspect, a theory which only deals with the second, and a theory which covers both (Table 4).

Table 4. A possible classification of multi-person decision theories.

	Individual preference orderings	Informational aspects
Group decision theory	Different	Not considered
Team theory	Equal	Considered
N-person game theory	Different	Considered

The theory which only considers how to obtain one single (group) preference ordering out of different individual preference orderings is called group decision theory (Arrow 1951). Differences in the information available to the various decision-makers are not considered in this theory.

The theory which only considers how to structure the information from which the individual decision-makers have to decide, in order to optimise the results of the decision process, is called 'team theory' (Marschak and Radner 1972). In this theory it is assumed that each individual in the group pursues the same common group values.

The theory in which both aspects are covered is the general n-person game theory (Von Neumann and Morgenstern 1944, Luce and Raiffa 1957). n-person game theory can be further subdivided into:

1. The number of decision-makers considered, namely two persons or n persons ($n > 2$). Although the n-person theory should be of greater interest in fields of application such as economics and sociology, the two-person theory has been much further elaborated in the mathematical sense; mathematically neat and general n-person theories present many more difficulties.

2. The kind of preference ordering. Are the interests of the decision-makers strictly opposite in that what one wins the other loses (zero sum), or can we not speak of strictly opposing interests (non-zero sum).

3. The presence or absence of pre-play communication to make joint agreements. In two-person games this leads to a sub-division into co-operative and non-cooperative games. In n-person games ($n > 2$) the formation of coalitions among players is one of the main topics of the theory.

Of course this classification is one of many possibilities – see, for example, the classification of contexts for n-person games in Luce and Raiffa (1957: chapter 7.7).

In order to show the essential contents and the main differences between the three theories already mentioned, we will present the three formal models.

A team decision consists of:

– a set of n individuals, denoted by 1, 2, ... n;

– a set of alternatives, A. The action $a_i \in A$ of the i-th person is related to the information y_i available to that person: $a_i = \alpha_i(y_i)$. The n-tuple of decision functions $\alpha = (\alpha_1 \ . \ . \ . \ \alpha_n)$ is called the decision rule of the team. The information variable y_i is in its turn related to the true state of the world x by a function: $y_i = \eta_i(x)$, thus $a_i = \alpha_i[\eta_i(x)]$. The n-tuple $\eta = (\eta_1 \ . \ . \ . \ \eta_n)$ is called the information structure of the team;

– a gross pay-off function $u = w(x, a_1, a_2...)$ denoting the utility to the team. This function can be rewritten as

$$u = w(x, a) = w(x, \alpha[\eta(x)]) = w(x, \alpha_1[\eta_1(x)], \ldots, \alpha_n[\eta_n(x)]);$$
– the team should maximise the expectation of the pay-off function.

A n-person game consists of:
– a set of n players, denoted by $1, 2, \ldots n$;
– n strategy sets $S_1, S_2 \ldots S_n$;
– n real-valued utility functions $M_1, M_2 \ldots, M_n$ where $M_i(s_1, s_2 \ldots s_n)$ is the utility to player i where player 1 uses strategy $s_1 \in S_1$, player 2 uses $s_2 \in S_2, \ldots$ and player n uses $s_n \in S_n$;
– each player attempts to maximise his (expected) utility.

A group decision consists of:
– a set of n individuals, denoted by $1, 2 \ldots, n$;
– a set of alternatives $A = \{a_1 \ldots a_m\}$;
– n preference ordering sets $O_1, \ldots O_n$ in which for any alternatives a_i and a_j from set A either individual k prefers a_i to a_j, or individual k prefers a_j to a_i, or he is indifferent between a_i and a_j.
– a 'social choice' function $F: O_1 \times O_2 \times \ldots O_n \to O$ which associates to all individual preference orderings the preference ordering of the group itself;
– the group chooses the most prefered alternative.

Obviously the n-person game is much more general than the group decision in the sense that the latter only considers n orderings over a fixed set of alternatives. Philosophically speaking, the difference between the theories is that in the n-person game all players pursue strict personal gain (which does not prohibit them from forming coalitions, although everything is done to obtain maximum personal gain), whereas in the group decision model everyone still has different aims and values but does not pursue strict personal gain; the aim there is to reach one acceptable group objective. Team theory concentrates on the desired information structure.

In this section only the theory of group decision-making will be examined further. The main reason is that a fuzzy theory on group decisions exists, whereas a fuzzy theory on teams does not yet exist, and existing literature on fuzzy games is rather specialised and mathematical (Aubin 1974a, b, 1976). To present these fuzzy extensions of n-person games would require too much explanation. Although an extension of game theory by means of the concept of fuzzy orderings would probably be quite similar to the approach of fuzzy multi-criteria decisions described in Chapter four, it would fall outside the scope of this survey.

3.2 Fuzzy group decision theory

In this sub-section the contribution of fuzzy set theory to group decision-making will be described and discussed. This contribution will be accompanied by a short outline of the 'classical' theory on group decisions which arose mainly from Arrow's basic work on social choice (Arrow 1951). A comparison of both theories will be made.

As stated previously, the problem can be formalised as follows. Given a group of n decision makers $\{B_1 \ldots B_n\}$ and a set of m alternatives $A = \{a_1 \ldots a_m\}$, each decision maker B_k has a preference ordering O_k – which is a binary relation from $A \times A$ into $\{0, 1\}$ – over the alternatives. The problem is to find a consistent group ordering O_0 by means of a mapping $F : O_1 \times O_2 \times \ldots \times O_n \rightarrow O_0$.

The argument for introducing fuzziness here is as follows (Blin 1974, Blin and Whinston 1974). Choosing between alternatives presupposes a preference ordering. This preference ordering is mathematically described as a reflexive, antisymmetric, and transitive binary relationship $O : A \times A \rightarrow \{0, 1\}$. Although individuals sometimes appear inconsistent in their preferences, one might say that this concept of ordering satisfies the case of an individual decision-maker.

However, the assumption that group ordering and group choice are always clearly defined and consistent is definitely not valid. It might even be argued that this case of a multiple opinion about a preference ordering is one of the clearest examples of the notion of fuzziness when compared with the notion of probability. Hence we define the social preference as a fuzzy relation on $A \times A$ with a membership function μ_R which associates to each pair $(a_i, a_j) \in A \times A$ its grade of membership $\mu_R(a_i, a_j)$ in the social preference ordering R:

$$\mu_R : A \times A \rightarrow [0, 1].$$

In Blin (1974) and Blin and Whinston (1974) some examples of 'social preference' membership functions are given.

Let O_k be the individual preference ordering of person k. Let $\sigma_{ij} = \{O_k | a_i \underset{k}{>} a_j\}$ be the set of individual preference orderings in which a_i is preferred to a_j, and let $N(\sigma_{ij})$ denote the number of elements in this set. Clearly $N(\sigma_{ij})$ denotes the number of persons who prefer a_i to a_j. Then some possible membership function assignments are:

$$\mu_{R_1}(a_i, a_j) = \frac{1}{n} N(\sigma_{ij})$$

or:

$$\mu_{R_2}(a_i, a_j) = \begin{cases} \frac{1}{n}[N(\sigma_{ij}) - N(\sigma_{ji})] & \text{for } N(\sigma_{ij}) > N(\sigma_{ji}) \\ 0 & \text{for } N(\sigma_{ij}) \leq N(\sigma_{ji}) \end{cases}$$

or:

$$\mu_{R_3}(a_i, a_j) = \begin{cases} 1 & \text{if } a_i \underset{k}{>} a_j & \text{for some individual } k \\ 0 & \text{if } a_j \underset{k}{>} a_i & \text{for some individual } k. \end{cases}$$

R_3 is an extreme case where all individuals but one have no group influence at all. Moreover R_3 is simply a non-fuzzy binary ordering.

By means of an α-level set R_α of a fuzzy relationship R_1 which is defined as a (non-fuzzy) set on $A \times A$

$$R_\alpha = \{ (a_i, a_j) | \mu_{R_1}(a_i, a_j) \geq \alpha \}$$

and since a fuzzy relationship can be divided into its α-level sets

$$R = \underset{\alpha}{\cup} \alpha R_\alpha \qquad\qquad 0 < \alpha \leq 1$$

where $\cup$ stands for the union and αR_α stands for the fuzzy set defined by:

$$\mu_{\alpha R_\alpha}(a_i, a_j) = \begin{cases} \alpha & \text{for } (a_i, a_j) \in R_\alpha \\ 0 & \text{elsewhere} \end{cases}$$

a procedure to obtain a final (non-fuzzy) group decision from the (fuzzy) 'social preference' can now be defined. For it should be noticed that a final group decision should have an essentially binary, non-fuzzy (yes or no) character.

The proposed procedure interprets the concept of an α-level as an 'agreement level' in the group. An α-level set consists of a certain preference ordering for which the level of acceptance or rejection in the group – α –

has not yet been surpassed. The lower the α-level, the lower the level of agreement of all individuals in the group to accept this certain (binary) preference ordering.

The following procedure is proposed in Blin (1974) for obtaining the final group choice:

1. Construct $R_{\alpha=1} = \{(a_i, a_j) \mid \mu_R(a_i, a_j) = 1\}$.
2. Find the ordering C_1 compatible with the pairs found in 1. (This ordering can easily be proved to form a partial ordering over A).
3. Construct the α-level set R_α with the next lower level (e.g. one might take $\alpha = 1.0, 0.9, 0.8 \ldots$).
4. Find the total ordering compatible with the pairs added in step 3 to the pairs found before (starting from the $\alpha = 1.0$ level).
5. If a pair (a_i, a_j) yields an intransitivity, remove it.
6. If the ordering is not yet complete, return to step 3, otherwise stop.

This procedure maximises the level of agreement:

$$\sum_{(ai,aj)\in I} \mu_R(a_i, a_j)$$

where I denotes:

$$I = \{(a_i, a_j) \in A \times A \mid \mu_R(a_i, a_j) < 1\}.$$

A major advantage of this particular procedure is that a group choice is attained which contains a certain level of agreement, namely that α where the ordering is complete.

We shall illustrate this procedure with an example from Blin and Whinston (1974). Suppose we have the set of alternatives $A = \{a, b, c, d\}$ and 10 decision-makers. Suppose that their preference orderings are:

$$O_1 = O_2 = (a, b, c, d)$$
$$O_3 = O_4 = (b, c, a, d)$$
$$O_5 = O_6 = O_7 = (d, a, b, c)$$
$$O_8 = (d, b, a, c)$$
$$O_9 = O_{10} = (d, c, a, b).$$

Using the membership function assignment:

$$\mu_{R1}(a_i, a_j) = \frac{1}{n} N(\sigma_{ij})$$

this gives the following fuzzy social preference matrix:

$$\mu_{R1} = \begin{bmatrix} 0 & 0.7 & 0.6 & 0.4 \\ 0.3 & 0 & 0.8 & 0.4 \\ 0.4 & 0.2 & 0 & 0.4 \\ 0.6 & 0.6 & 0.6 & 0 \end{bmatrix}$$

We now construct the level-sets starting from $\alpha = 1$:

$R_{\alpha=1} = \emptyset$

$R_{\alpha=.8} = \{(b, c)\}$

$R_{\alpha=.7} = \{(a, b); (b, c)\}$

$R_{\alpha=.6} = \{(a, b); (a, c); (b, c); (d, a); (d, b); (d, c)\}$

$R_{\alpha=.4} = \{(a, b); (a, c); (a, d); (b, c); (b, d); (c, d); (c, a); (d, a); (d, b); (d, c)\}$

$R_{\alpha=.3} = \{(a, b); (a, c); (a, d); (b, c); (b, d); (c, d); (b, a); (c, a); (d, a); (d, b); (d, c)\}$

$R_{a=.2} = \{(a, b); (a, c); (a, d); (b, c); (b, d); (c, d); (b, a); (c, a); (c, b); (d, a); (d, b); (d, c)\}$

which can be represented by the corresponding relation matrices:

$$R_{\alpha=.2} = \begin{bmatrix} 0 & 1 & 1 & 1 \\ 1 & 0 & 1 & 1 \\ 1 & 1 & 0 & 1 \\ 1 & 1 & 1 & 0 \end{bmatrix} ; R_{\alpha=.3} = \begin{bmatrix} 0 & 1 & 1 & 1 \\ 1 & 0 & 1 & 1 \\ 1 & 0 & 0 & 1 \\ 1 & 1 & 1 & 0 \end{bmatrix} ; R_{\alpha=.4} = \begin{bmatrix} 0 & 1 & 1 & 1 \\ 0 & 0 & 1 & 1 \\ 1 & 0 & 0 & 1 \\ 1 & 1 & 1 & 0 \end{bmatrix}$$

$$R_{\alpha=.6} = \begin{bmatrix} 0 & 1 & 1 & 0 \\ 0 & 0 & 1 & 0 \\ 0 & 0 & 0 & 0 \\ 1 & 1 & 1 & 0 \end{bmatrix} ; R_{\alpha=.7} = \begin{bmatrix} 0 & 1 & 0 & 0 \\ 0 & 0 & 1 & 0 \\ 0 & 0 & 0 & 0 \\ 0 & 0 & 0 & 0 \end{bmatrix} ; R_{\alpha=.8} = \begin{bmatrix} 0 & 0 & 0 & 0 \\ 0 & 0 & 1 & 0 \\ 0 & 0 & 0 & 0 \\ 0 & 0 & 0 & 0 \end{bmatrix}$$

The procedure for obtaining the group choice from the original relation matrix R_1 can now be easily illustrated. In order to help to find and remove intransitivities we use a diagram in which an arrow corresponds to a binary preference relationship (figure 9).

Iteration 1: Construct $R_{\alpha=1}$

Iteration 2: Construct $R_{\alpha=0.8}$

Iteration 3: Construct $R_{\alpha=0.7}$

Iteration 4: Construct $R_{\alpha=0.6}$

The ordering is complete.

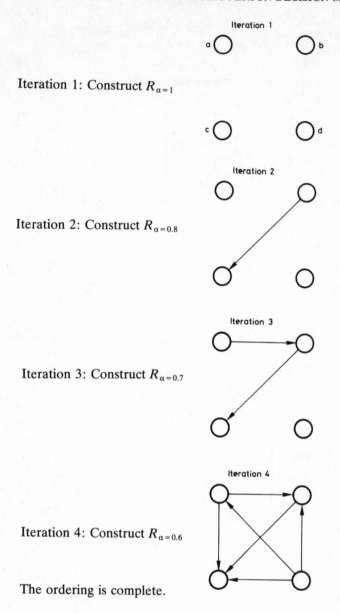

Fig. 9. The construction of a group ordering.

3.3. Fuzzy and non-fuzzy group decision theory: the Arrow paradox

We shall now try to establish some relationships between this procedure and the well-known group decision problems such as Arrow's paradox. This paradox states that the following set of conditions to the group decision problem form an inconsistent set (Arrow 1951, Luce and Raiffa 1957):

- collective rationality: this condition can be sub-divided into:
  - the number m of elements in $A = \{a_1 \ldots a_m\}$ is greater or equal to three: $m \geq 3$.
  - the number n of individuals in $\{B_1 \ldots B_n\}$ is greater or equal to two: $n \geq 2$.
  - the social choice mapping $F : O_1 \times \ldots \times O_m \rightarrow O_0$ is defined for all possible $(O_1 \ldots O_m) \in O^m$.
- Pareto optimality: if $a_i \underset{k}{>} a_j$ for each individual k, this should hold for the group preference too.
- independence of irrelevant alternatives: let A_1 be any subset of A, hence $A_1 \subset A$. If the individual preference orderings are modified with the restriction that each individual's paired comparisons among the alternatives of A_1 are left invariant, the social group ordering for the alternatives in A_1 should remain identical.
- non-dictatorship: there is no individual k such that whenever $a_i \underset{k}{>} a_j$ (for any $a_i, a_j \in A$) the group does likewise, regardless of the other individuals.

Arrow proved that no social choice function exists which possesses the properties demanded by these four conditions.

Some group decision rules

We shall briefly discuss some four methods of social choice, of which the first two only presuppose a preference ordering, whereas the latter two methods restrict the allowed individual preference profiles in the sense that the preference orderings should be measured on a metric scale (interval property).

Simple majority rule

The most obvious and intuitively right rule is the simple majority rule. Let $\sigma_{ij} = \{O_k | a_i \underset{k}{>} a_j\}$ and let $N(\sigma_{ij})$ be the number of elements in this set. The group preference ordering O_0: $A \times A \to \{0, 1\}$ then becomes

$$\{O_0 | a_i > a_j\} \text{ if } N(\sigma_{ij}) > \frac{n}{2}.$$

It can be shown that, if very dissimilar individual orderings are permitted, this rule can lead to an intransitive set of social preferences.

Copeland's rule

A rule which by-passes the problem of intransitivity in the simple majority rule is to choose such that:

$$\{O_0 | a_i > a_j\} \text{ if } \sum_{k=1}^{m} N(\sigma_{ik}) - \sum_k N(\sigma_{ki}) > \sum_k N(\sigma_{jk}) - \sum_k N(\sigma_{kj}).$$

However, this rule does not meet the condition of independence of irrelevant alternatives.

Sum and product rule

Given a preference ordering measured on an interval scale, which means that the value function $\Psi_k(a_i)$, $i = 1, 2 \ldots m$ – related to the ordering O_k of $\{a_1 \ldots a_m\}$ – is known apart from zero and unity, the group ordering can be reached in the following ways. If the unities β_k of the value functions Ψ_k are known, but not the zeros of α_k, then apply the sum-rule:

$$\Psi_o(a_i) = \sum_{k=1}^{n} \Psi_k(a_i)/\beta_k \qquad\qquad i = 1, 2 \ldots m; \, \beta_k \in R^+.$$

If on the contrary the zeros α_k are known but not the unities β_k, then we use the product-rule

$$\Psi_0(a_i) = \prod_{k=1}^{n} [\Psi_k(a_i) - \alpha_k] \qquad\qquad i = 1, 2, \ldots m; \, \alpha_k \in R.$$

The group preference ordering thus obtained possesses the property of invariance to linear scale transformations of individual orderings.

Fuzzy and non-fuzzy group decisions

The application of the (fuzzy) social preference procedure to a membership function of the form:

$$\mu_R(a_i, a_j) = \frac{1}{n} N(\sigma_{ij})$$

amounts to the simple majority rule. It is therefore easy to conclude that this rule may lead to intransitivities. An example given in Blin and Whinston (1974) shows that the procedure also results in intransitivity if the membership function:

$$\mu_R(a_i, a_j) = \begin{cases} \dfrac{1}{n} [N(\sigma_{ij}) - N(\sigma_{ji})] & \text{for } N(\sigma_{ij}) > N(\sigma_{ji}) \\ \\ 0 & \text{for } N(\sigma_{ij}) \leqq N(\sigma_{ji}) \end{cases}$$

is used. The third proposed membership function

$$\mu_R(a_i, a_k) = \begin{cases} 1 & \text{if } a_i > a_j \quad \text{for some } k \\ 0 & \text{elsewhere} \end{cases}$$

obviously violates the last condition of Arrow's paradox. Blin recognises the problem of transitivity in his papers and emphasises the importance of imposing conditions on the fuzzy ordering relationship in order to ensure transitivity. Generally a fuzzy relationship is defined as transitive if

$$\mu_R(a_i, a_k) \geqq \max_{aj} \min \{\mu_R(a_i, a_j); \mu_R(a_j, a_k)\}$$

with $a_i, a_j, a_k \in A = \{a_1 \ldots a_m\}$.

One way to obtain a transitive fuzzy relationship from any fuzzy relationship is to construct the transitive closure of a relationship (Kaufmann 1973). Let R be a fuzzy relationship on $X \times X$, then

$$R^2 = R \circ R$$

is defined by

$$\mu_{R2}(x, z) = \max_{y} \min [\mu_R(x, y); \mu_R(y, z)]$$

where $x, y, z \in X$. The transitivity condition can be written as:

$R \circ R \subset R$

and hence

$$R^{k+1} \subset R^k \qquad\qquad\qquad\qquad\qquad k = 1, 2 \ldots$$

Now the transitive closure of a fuzzy binary relationship, denoted by $\hat{R}$, is defined by:

$$\hat{R} = R \cup R^2 \cup R^3 \cup \ldots$$

If above a certain k

$$R^{k+1} = R^k$$

then the transitive closure becomes a finite sum

$$\hat{R} = R \cup R^2 \cup \ldots \cup R^k.$$

This is the case when R is a fuzzy relationship on $X \times X$ where X is a finite set with card $(X) = k$, and where the diagonal elements of R are all one.

3.4. An axiomatic approach to rational group decision-making

In Fung and Fu (1975) a different approach to the group decision problem is presented. They view the problem as finding a rational way to aggregate individual preferences in one consistent group preference pattern. They postulate seven conditions which such an aggregation must satisfy before being accepted, and from there derive the aggregation which satisfies them.

Suppose we have a set of alternative actions A, then the preference pattern of each individual is represented by a fuzzy set on A where $\mu_i (a)$ denotes the degree of preference of action $a \in A$ by individual i, $\mu_i : A \rightarrow [0, 1]$. If for every $a \in A$, $\mu_i(a) > \mu_j(a)$, then we can say that individual i prefers action a more than individual j does.

The membership of alternative action a represents the degree of accepitibility of the action to the individuals in the group. Another interpretation of the fuzzy set is as follows. Individual i constructs his admissible set A_i by assigning preferences $\mu_i(a)$ to every action $a \in A$, with $\mu_i(a) \in [0, 1]$. Then the admissible set can be represented by a fuzzy set A_i with membership function $\mu_i : A \rightarrow [0, 1]$. In the axiomatic approach the $[0, 1]$ interval, which is the usual range of membership functions, is replaced by a topological structure S induced by a linear order $\leq$. A set S is a linearly ordered set if there is a linear order $\leq$ on S satisfying the four conditions:

1. $x \leq x$ for every $x \in S$.
2. if $x \leq y$ and $y \leq x$, then $x = y$.
3. if $x \leq y$ and $y \leq z$, then $x \leq z$.
4. for each pair $x, y \in S$ either $x \leq y$ or $y \leq x$.

The aggregate of the fuzzy sets representing the individual preferences is taken to represent the preference pattern of the whole group. The group chooses that action which has the highest membership in the aggregate set. A list of seven basic assumptions on the properties of a rational group aggregate will be given, from which the particular forms of aggregates will be deduced.

Definition

Let F be the class of fuzzy sets on a set of actions A taking values in a range S. An aggregation $\oplus$ is a binary operation on F, $\oplus : F \times F \rightarrow F$; and an aggregate of two fuzzy sets $A_1, A_2 \in F$ is denoted by $A_1 \oplus A_2$.

Axiom I: law of independent components
There exists a function $\bullet : S \times S \rightarrow S$ such that:

$$A_1 \oplus A_2 = \{(a, \mu_{A_1}(a) \bullet \mu_{A_2}(a)) : a \in A\}$$

This axiom states that the membership of an aggregate depends only on the membership of the constituent fuzzy sets.

Axiom II: idempotent law
For all $A \in F : A \oplus A = A$.

Axiom III: commutative law
For all $A, B \in F : A \oplus B = B \oplus A$.

Axiom IV
For $m \geq 3$ define $A_1 \oplus A_2 \oplus \ldots \oplus A_m$ inductively by:
$A_1 \oplus \ldots \oplus A_m = (A_1 \oplus \ldots \oplus A_{m-1}) \oplus A_m$.

Axiom V: associative law
For all $A, B, C \in F$: $A \oplus (B \oplus C) = (A \oplus B) \oplus C$.

The last three axioms together imply that an aggregate for $m \geq 2$ is invariant for any permutation of the subscripts $i, \ldots, m$.

Axiom VI: non-decreasingness of $\oplus$
For any action $a \in A$ and fuzzy sets $B, C_1, C_2 \in F$ with $A_1 = B \oplus C_1$ and $A_2 = B \oplus C_2$: if $\mu_{C_1}(a) > \mu_{C_2}(a)$ then $\mu_{A_1}(a) > \mu_{A_2}(a)$.

This system of axioms leads to the following theorem.

Theorem I
Let S be a connected order topological space induced by a linear order $\leq$. Suppose the definition and axioms hold. Then for every a and b in S we can either have:

$$a \bullet b = \min[a, b] \qquad \text{(pessimistic)}$$

or:

$$a \bullet b = \max[a, b] \qquad \text{(optimistic)}$$

or the aggregate is of the mixed type.
An aggregate of the mixed type is a binary operator $\bullet$ such that:

$$z_1 \bullet z_2 = x \text{ for } z_1 \leq x \text{ and } z_2 \geq x$$
$$z_1 \bullet z_2 = \max[z_1, z_2] \text{ for } z_1, z_2 \leq x$$
$$z_1 \bullet z_2 = \min[z_1, z_2] \text{ for } z_1, z_2 \geq x$$

where x is some arbitrary fixed threshold point.
   Moreover, if we replace Axiom VI (non-decreasingness) by:

Axiom VII

There exists a point α in S and a lower limit of S, denoted by O, such that for all x, $0 \leq x < \alpha$: $O \bullet x = O$

then $\oplus$ must be a pessimistic aggregate.

If we replace Axiom VI by:

Axiom VIII

there exists a point β in S and an upper limit of S, denoted by I, such that for all x, $\beta < x \leq 1 : I \bullet x = I$

then $\oplus$ must be an optimistic aggregate.

Note that this axiomatic approach can serve two purposes. It is a deduction of the form that an aggregation of individual preferences into one group preference must have. On the other hand, if we are interested in the derivation of the intersection and union operations of fuzzy sets, it gives the conditions under which the maximum and minimum operators hold good.

3.5. Discussion

Two approaches to constructing fuzzy theories on group decision-making have been presented. In the first the reason for introducing fuzziness into group decisions is very credible and convincing. However, the main problem in group decision-making is how to obtain a group decision from different individual orderings in such a way that some rational criteria are satisfied. This problem is overlooked in the sense that the particular assignments of the 'social preference' membership function in fact amount to exactly the same as conventional methods and thus have the same defects. Rather than solving many problems, the theory looks more like a proposal for an appealing procedure for assigning membership functions.

The second approach is an axiomatic treatment of rational group decision-making based on the definition of an individual preference as a fuzzy set. This leads to a mathematically elegant derivation of the form the group aggregate should have. This approach differs from the first, where the group preference is a fuzzy set, since here the individual preferences are already fuzzy sets. However, the practical relevance of the second approach is not clear. The practical meanings of the several assumptions in terms of actual group decisions are not explained. A translation of these assumptions into the usual rationality assumptions is missing. It would be interesting to see what the implications of a minimum or maximum aggregation rule are in terms of the criteria for democratic group decisionmaking as formulated by Arrow (1951). Rather than showing which practical problems are solved by its use, this second approach looks more like a procedure for determining the form of fuzzy union and intersection connectives.

4. Fuzzy multi-criteria decision-making

4.1. Introduction

A kind of decision problem which is different but in a certain sense also related to multi-person decision-making is the problem of multi-criteria decision-making. The situation here is that all the alternatives in the choice set can be evaluated according to a number of criteria. The problem is to construct an evaluation procedure to rank the set of alternatives in order of preference. The multi-criteria decision problem is usually described as:

- a set of alternatives $A = \{a_1 \ldots a_m\}$.
- a set of n criteria, denoted by $1, 2 \ldots n$.
- n preference ordering sets $O_1, \ldots, O_n$ in which O_k stands for the ordering of the alternatives according to the k-th criterion:

$$O_k : A \times A \rightarrow \{0, 1\}$$

resulting in the ordered set:

$$\{a_{k1}, a_{k2}, \ldots a_{km}\}$$

which is a permutation of $A = \{a_1 \ldots a_m\}$.
- a set of weights $W = \{w_1 \ldots w_n\}$ where w_k denotes the importance of criterion k in the evaluation of the alternatives.

Apart from the set of weights, this representation of the problem clearly shows its similarity to the group decision model.

In this chapter two approaches to the multi-criteria problem thus formulated will be presented (Sections 4.2 and 4.4). We shall show the differences between these methods both in theory and in applicability, emphasising the applicability. Between these two presentations a short diversion will be made to show a rather different way of multi-criteria decision-making (Section 4.3).

In Section 4.5 the multi-criteria problem is not formulated in the above-mentioned sense but as a linear programming problem with several objectives. We will show that the framework of a fuzzy decision (Section 2.2) which is in fact adopted in that approach implies a particular aggregation of criteria, namely equal weights and minimum composition, instead of the usual different weights and additive composition such as presented in Section 4.4.

4.2. Aggregation of criteria

The first approach to the multi-criteria decision problem to be sketched here is presented by Kaufmann in the third book of his series on fuzzy sets (Kaufmann 1975b: chapter 87). Although Kaufmann does not explicitly state the problem in the terms we have used and admits that he only gives a rather chaotic summary of methods of criteria aggregation, he presents a very elegant way in which to introduce the concept of a fuzzy set in this area.

The approach starts with an abstract definition of a criterion; indeed the defining factor of the whole approach is this definition of a criterion:

A criterion $C(X)$ on a set X is defined as that which establishes a structure on this set.

This structure may be defined by a mapping of $X \times X$ into $\{0, 1\}$, which gives a binary relationship that can represent an ordering, a lattice, etc. A second way to define this structure is to represent it by a mapping from X into a set L which possesses a configuration of ordering, lattice, etc. This latter definition is precisely the definition of an L-fuzzy set (Goguen 1967). Thus by definition an L-fuzzy set constitutes a criterion on X. Representing all possible L-fuzzy (sub)sets on X by L^X, we can now state that

$$C(X) \in L^X.$$

If we confine the set L to the closed zero-one interval, we obtain fuzzy sets in the usual sense of Zadeh (1965a).

The notion of weighting – different levels of importance of the various criteria – can also be embedded in the theory of fuzzy sets. Consider a support set X and let $L = [0, 1]$, then the set of order criteria M will be a subset of L^X:

$$M = \{C^1(x), C^2(x), \ldots C^m(x)\} \subset L^X$$

with

$$C^i(x) \in L^X, \qquad\qquad\qquad\qquad i = 1, 2 \ldots m.$$

Given M and a set Π of m weights $\Pi = \{p_1, p_2 \ldots p_m\}, p_i \in [0, 1]$, then the fuzzy set $\underset{\sim}{M}$ on M defined by:

$$\begin{aligned}\mu_{\underset{\sim}{M}}(C^i(x)) &= p_i && \text{if } C^i \in M \\ &= 0 && \text{if } C^i \notin M\end{aligned}$$

is called the 'weighting of the order criteria'.

If moreover $\overset{m}{\underset{i=1}{\Sigma}} p_i = 1$ the weighting will be called 'normal'.

Note that:

$$\underset{\sim}{M} \in L^{(L^X)}.$$

The problem of aggregation of criteria is represented by Kaufmann in the following manner.

Let X be a (finite) set and M a set of L-fuzzy sets on X: $M = \{A_1, A_2 \ldots A_m\}$ with $A_i : X \to L$ (e.g. $L = [0, 1]$). Then the problem consists of finding an ordering over these m L-fuzzy sets.

In Kaufmann (1975b: chapter 87) this aggregation problem is further sub-divided into two situations: either L possesses cardinal properties (scale unknown apart from zero and unity), or L only possesses ordinal properties (ordered scale). We shall here present only that method which is closest to the classical method.

Let X be $X = \{x_1 \ldots x_n\}$ and suppose one has m fuzzy sets $M = \{A_1 \ldots A_m\}$ on X, characterised by their membership functions $\mu_{A_i}(x_j), j = 1, \ldots n$; $i = 1, \ldots m$. Assume a set of weights $\Pi = \{p_1, p_2 \ldots p_n\}$. Then calculate:

$$v(A_i) = \overset{n}{\underset{j=1}{\Sigma}} \mu_{A_i}(x_j) \cdot p_j.$$

These $v(A_i)$ will induce an ordering over the fuzzy sets A_i.

Instead of considering this method *per se*, we shall first give an example of an application which uses a simpler version of this aggregation approach.

Application

In Van Velthoven (1975) fuzzy multi-criteria methods are applied to personnel management problems. The specific problem considered is that of the recruitment and selection of personnel. This selection of candidates is performed by comparing the candidate profiles $P_1 \ldots P_n$ with the required profile P_0 taking into account a certain number of criteria $C_1 \ldots C_m$ (see Table 5).

Table 5. Required and candidate profiles.

	C_1,	$C_2 \ldots$	C_m
P_0	p_1^0,	$p_2^0 \ldots$	p_m^0
P_1	p_1^1,	$p_2^1 \ldots$	p_m^1
$\vdots$	$\vdots$	$\vdots$	$\vdots$
P_n	p_1^n,	$p_2^n \ldots$	p_m^n

In the non-fuzzy approach the ranking of candidate j to criterion $i : p_j^i$, is either zero or one.

Several methods of evaluations the rankings can be used, for example:

1. Vector product:

$$q^j = \sum_{i=1}^{m} p_i^0 \, p_i^j$$

which expresses the number of required criteria that are satisfied.

2. Vector product with complementary vector:

$$q^j = \sum_{i=1}^{m} p_j^0 p_i^j + \sum_{i=1}^{m} (1 - p_i^0) \, (1 - p_i^j),$$

which expresses the number of characteristics in common with the required profile.

3. Complementary Hamming distance

$$q^j = 1 - \frac{1}{m} \sum_{i=1}^{m} |p^0_i - p^j_i|.$$

This is the normalised version of the previous version in the case of non-fuzzy profiles.

4. Similarity index

$$q^j = 1 - \frac{\sum\limits_{i=1}^{m} |p^0_i - p^j_i|}{m + \sum\limits_{i=1}^{m} p^0_i p^j_i}$$

which expresses the similarity to the required profile.

There is a straightforward extension of this recruitment selection method into a fuzzy method. The profiles are now considered to be fuzzy sets P_i on the same support set $\{C_1 \ldots C_m\}$

$$P_i = \{C_1|\mu^i_1; C_2|\mu^i_2 \ \ldots \ C_m|\mu^i_m\} \qquad \mu^i_j \in [0, 1].$$

The selection procedures can be easily extended for this fuzzy case. However, it should be noted that the 'vector product' procedure and the 'vector product with complementary vector' procedure lose their significance because they no longer indicate numbers. The only remaining valuable selection procedures are the complementary Hamming distance:

$$q^j = 1 - \frac{1}{m} \sum_{i=1}^{m} |\mu^0_i - \mu^j_i|$$

and the similarity index:

$$q^j = 1 - \frac{\delta[P_0; P_j]}{m + [P_0 \cap P_j]} = 1 - \frac{\sum\limits_{i=1}^{m} |\mu^0_i - \mu^j_i|}{m + \sum\limits_{i=1}^{m} \mu^0_i \wedge \mu^j_i}$$

An additional method that can be used to classify the candidates is the 'outranking' method: the candidate profile P_i outranks P_j if

$c_{ij} \geq c$ and
$d_{ij} > d$

where c_{ij} is the relative number of membership functions yielding

$$|\mu_i - \mu_0| \leq |\mu_j - \mu_0|$$

and

$$d_{ij} = \sup\left[|\mu_j - \mu_0| - |\mu_i - \mu_0|\right] \text{ if } d_{ij} > 0 \text{ otherwise } 0.$$

The lower the required c and the higher the required d-level, the smaller the number of non-outranked candidates.

According to Van Velthoven (1975) the fuzzy set approach divides into four fundamental steps:

1. Define an adequate support set (referential set) for the fuzzy characteristics, for example the seven-element support:

$$\text{height} \begin{cases} \nearrow \text{tall} \\ - \text{medium} \\ \searrow \text{small} \end{cases}$$

$$\text{sex} \begin{cases} \nearrow \text{m} \\ \searrow \text{f} \end{cases}$$

$$\text{intelligence} \begin{cases} \nearrow \text{very intelligent} \\ \searrow \text{intelligent} \end{cases}$$

2. Define the membership functions of the required profile P_0: for example, $P_0 = \{\text{tall}/0.8; \text{medium}/0.7; \text{small}/0.0; \text{m}/1.00; \text{f}/0.00; \text{very intelligent}/0.1; \text{intelligent}/0.7\}$.
3. Find the membership functions of the candidate profiles $P_1 \ldots P_m$. According to Van Velthoven (1975), this may be done by classical psychometric methods and by fuzzifying the resulting characteristics.
4. Compute the selection indices to obtain the final classification.

Discussion

The reason that the application of Van Velthoven (1975) has been considered after the presentation of the fuzzy multi-criteria method of Kaufmann (1975b) is as follows. Although the reader will have noticed that in the personnel recruitment problem no weights were used for the criteria and that the evaluation procedures proposed there were not so simple as the calculation of:

$$\nu\ (A_i) = \sum_{j=1}^{n} \mu_{A_i}(x_j) \cdot p_j$$

as proposed by Kaufmann (1975b), there is one important similarity between both methods: the ranking of an alternative A_i according to a criterion x_j is represented by one fuzzy membership value $\mu_{A_i}(x_j) \in [0, 1]$ (or μ_j^i in the case of the profiles). In that sense the 'fuzzy' ranking looks rather like a conventional ranking coefficient, be it only that the fuzzy one is normalised into the interval $[0, 1]$. This characteristic of the fuzzy ranking is quite surprising when we see that Van Velthoven (1975) proposed using 'tall', 'medium', 'small', etc. as support sets on which to determine membership values. Usually terms like these are considered standard examples of fuzzy sets themselves. What we would expect of fuzzy ranking coefficients is that these coefficients themselves are fuzzy sets rather than just a single membership function. This is surely the case where ranking can only be given in terms like 'good', 'very good', etc. It is hard to imagine what kind of fuzziness is meant when the decision-maker is still able to assign a numerical rating coefficient.

Before we proceed with a method which indeed represents ratings and weights by fuzzy sets (Section 4.4) we shall first take a side-track and briefly present a totally different way of aggregating criteria.

4.3. A different way of aggregating criteria

Quite apart from the usual methods of aggregating criteria, the problem can be viewed as a clustering problem. This is done in the following way. In the set of alternatives some measure of similarity or dissimilarity (distance) is defined. The ranking of alternatives is then replaced by finding clusters of similar, ressemblant alternatives. The clusters can then be ordered according to the index of resemblance that is achieved.

Several authors have considered the problem in this way. In Vincke (1973) the clustering of alternatives is treated by means of similarity indices and is more generally based on the theory of graphs. In Roy (1975) several methods of aggregating criteria with and without fuzzy sets are outlined, in particular the fuzzy outranking concept. In this sub-section we shall only present one method proposed by Kaufmann (1975b, chapter 87) in order to show the general lines of the approach.

Let us start by defining some concepts which will be used in the approach.

A distance is defined as a mapping D from $X \times X$ into R^+ satisfying the following four conditions

1. $\forall (x, y) \in X^2 : D(x, y) \geq 0$.
2. $\forall (x, y) \in X^2 : x = y \Leftrightarrow D(x, y) = 0$.
3. $\forall (x, y) \in X^2 : D(x, y) = D(y, x)$.
4. $\forall (x, y), (y, z), (x, z) \in X^2 : D(x, z) \leq \bigwedge_y (D(x, y) * D(y, z))$.

Hence distance is an anti-reflexive, symmetric, and (min-star) transitive binary relation. If the star operation ($*$) is replaced by the maximum operation ($\vee$), the distance is called an ultra-metric. This notion of distance can easily be extended to a notion of distances between fuzzy sets. Distance then applies to any two fuzzy sets A and B on X. Two examples are the Hamming distance:

$$D(A, B) = \sum_{i=1}^{n} |\mu_A(x_i) - \mu_B(x_i)|$$

and the Euclidean distance:

$$D(A, B) = \sqrt{\sum_{i=1}^{n} [\mu_A(x_i) - \mu_B(x_i)]^2}.$$

Both distances possess a min-sum transitivity:

$$D(x, z) \leq \bigwedge_y [D(x, y) + D(y, z)].$$

Hierarchy of fuzzy sets

Through the concept of distance we can now obtain an ordering over the set of alternatives. By calculating the distance $D(A_i, A_j)$ for all A_i, A_j we can construct a hierarchy of the fuzzy sets. Therefore we define a dissimilarity relation R characterised by its membership function:

$$\mu_R(A_i, A_j) = D(A_i, A_j).$$

By taking as the distance the generalised Hamming distance:

$$D(A, B) = \frac{1}{n} \sum_{i=1}^{n} |\mu_A(x_i) - \mu_B(x_i)|$$

we can satisfy $\mu_R \in [0, 1]$.

In order to obtain a well-structured hierarchy, it is advisable to form the (min-max) transitive closure of this dissimilarity relation R

$$\hat{R} = R \cup R^2 \cup R^3 \cup \ldots \cup R^m.$$

The hierarchy of fuzzy sets is now built up by grouping together the fuzzy sets having a dissimilarity smaller than α, with α increasing from zero to one. That is, form the subsets of the set:

$$H_\alpha = \{A_{i_1}, A_{i_2}, \ldots A_{i_k}\}$$

so that:

$$\mu_R(A_{ij}, A_{i_1}) \leq \alpha \qquad\qquad \forall\ A_{ij}, A_{i_1} \in H_\alpha$$

starting from $\alpha = 0$ and in increasing order of $\alpha \in [0, 1]$. This concept of hierarchy coincides with the notion of α-level sets of fuzzy sets. By means of this last notion one can construct an indexed hierarchy satisfying the following conditions: an indexed hierarchy H on $M = \{A_1 \ldots A_m\}$ is a subset of all possible fuzzy sets on X

$$H \subset L^X$$

with the following conditions:

1. Every single fuzzy set $A \in M$ belongs to H.
2. M belongs to H.
3. If two elements B and C of H have a non-empty intersection, either $B \subset C$ or $C \subset B$.
4. There exists an index $\varphi : H \to R^+$.
5. Every single fuzzy set A of H has an index $\varphi(A) = 0$.
6. If B contains C then $\varphi(B) \geq \varphi(C)$.

That this concept of indexed hierarchy can be realised by means of α-level sets can easily be verified, for

$$R_\alpha = \{M\} \quad \text{if } \alpha = 0$$

by the very definition of a fuzzy set, and

$$R_{\alpha_1} \supset R_{\alpha_2} \quad \text{if } \alpha_1 \leq \alpha_2.$$

4.4. Fuzzy rating and ranking of multi-criteria alternatives

A well-known way of multi-criteria decision-making is the procedure which calculates a weighted average rating. Given a set of alternatives $A = \{a_1 \ldots a_m\}$ and a set of n criteria, the merit of alternative a_i according to the criterion j is denoted by the rating r_{ij}. The relative importance of each criterion is denoted by a weight w_j. Then alternative a_i receives the weighted average rating

$$\bar{r}_i = \sum_{j=1}^{n} w_j r_{ij} \bigg/ \sum_{j=1}^{n} w_j.$$

This average rating now induces an ordering of the alternatives $a_1 \ldots a_m$.

In this approach it is assumed that the practical situation allows for an exact numerical representation of the various ratings and weights. However, many situations occur where this numerical representation (on a metric scale) is not allowed for; these situations are characterised by the small amount of precise information and the predominant uncertainty. Rating and weights can at most be described in terms such as 'good', 'bad', 'unimportant', etc.

It is argued by Baas and Kwakernaak (1975) that this sort of uncertainty lends itself excellently to description by means of fuzzy sets. In fact, their paper is a reaction to and a comparison with a recently proposed probabilistic method. In this method (Kahne 1975) the uncertainties are accounted for by the introduction of random variables for the ratings and weights. This probabilistic approach represents an assessment of the value 'good' for a certain aspect by a random variable uniformly distributed over a certain interval. In Kahne's approach all weights and ratings are random variables, usually but not necessarily uniformly distributed, so that the final ratings $\bar{r}_i$ also become random variables. The final evaluation of the alternatives is performed by selecting the alternative that has the highest probability of being the best. A Monte Carlo method is used to determine this alternative.

In Baas and Kwakernaak (1975) the following alternative procedure is proposed. Let $A_1, A_2, \ldots A_m$ denote the alternatives that are compared and $x_1, x_2, \ldots x_n$ the different criteria (aspects) on which the alternatives are judged. Assume a fuzzy rating to criterion x_j of alternative A_i, characterised by a membership function $\mu_{R_{ij}}(r_{ij})$ where $r_{ij} \in R$. Similarly the relative importance of criterion x_j will be a fuzzy variable as well, characterised by $\mu_{W_j}(w_j)$, where $w_j \in R^+$. All membership functions take values in the closed interval $[0, 1]$, all fuzzy sets are normal, and all support sets are finite.

Consider the function $g_i(z_i) : R^{2n} \to R$ defined by:

$$g_i(z_i) = \sum_{j=1}^{n} w_j r_{ij} \bigg/ \sum_{j=1}^{n} w_j$$

where $z_i = (w_1 \dots w_n, r_{i1} \dots r_{in})$. Define the membership function μ_{Z_i} by:

$$\mu_{Z_i}(z_i) = \bigwedge_{j=1}^{n} \mu_{W_j}(w_j) \bigwedge_{k=1}^{n} \mu_{R_{ik}}(r_{ik}).$$

Through the mapping $g_i : R^{2n} \to R$ the fuzzy set Z_i induces a fuzzy set R_i with membership function:

$$\mu_{R_i}(\bar{r}_i) = \sup_{z_i : g_i(z_i) = \bar{r}_i} \mu_{Z_i}(z_i), \bar{r}_i \in R.$$

This membership function characterises the final fuzzy rating of alternative A_i.

Fuzzy set induced by a mapping

The notion of a fuzzy set induced by a mapping requires some explanation. If there exists a mapping $f(x) = y, x \in X, y \in Y$ and a fuzzy set A on X, then the fuzzy set B on Y induced by A via the mapping f is defined by its membership function:

$$\mu_B(y) = \sup_{x : f(x) = y} \mu_A(x).$$

If there exists a mapping $f : X_1 \times X_2 \times \dots \times X_n \to Y$ and n fuzzy sets $A_1, \dots A_n$ on $X_1, \dots X_n$ respectively, then the induced fuzzy set B is defined by:

$$\mu_B(y) = \sup_{(x_1 \dots x_n) : f(x_1, \dots x_n) = y} \bigwedge_{i=1}^{n} \mu_{A_i}(x_i).$$

This last definition is used in the procedure.

Final evaluation

Once the final fuzzy rating of the alternatives A_i, namely the fuzzy sets with membership functions $\mu_{R_i}(\bar{r}_i)$, have been calculated, the question arises how to select one single preferred alternative. As usual, the available information and the decision procedure may be fuzzy, the required actions are not.

The evaluation procedure proposed in Baas and Kwakernaak (1975) is rather unusual compared with the common choice of that alternative where the membership function is maximal. They propose the following. First define a conditional fuzzy set with membership function:

$$\mu_{I/R}(i|\bar{r}_1 \ldots \bar{r}_m) = 1 \text{ if } \bar{r}_i \geq \bar{r}_j \qquad\qquad \forall j \in \{1, 2 \ldots m\}$$
$$0 \text{ otherwise.}$$

Now construct the fuzzy set R with membership function:

$$\mu_R(\bar{r}_1, \bar{r}_2 \ldots \bar{r}_m) = \bigwedge_{i=1}^{m} \mu_{R_i}(\bar{r}_i).$$

This last fuzzy set, together with the conditional fuzzy set, induces a fuzzy set I with membership function

$$\mu_I(i) = \sup_{\bar{r}_1 \ldots \bar{r}_m} \mu_{I/R}(i|\bar{r}_1 \ldots \bar{r}_m) \wedge \mu_R(\bar{r}_1 \ldots \bar{r}_m)$$

$$= \sup_{\bar{r}_1 \ldots \bar{r}_m : \bar{r}_i \geq \bar{r}_j \forall_j} \bigwedge_{j=1}^{m} \mu_{R_j}(\bar{r}_j).$$

The membership value $\mu_I(i)$ is interpreted as a characterisation of the extent to which alternative A_i is the best available.

On first sight this procedure looks rather awkward. It should, however, be regarded as an application of the above-mentioned principle of an induction of a fuzzy set by a mapping. The corresponding mapping here is to select the alternative that has the highest final rating: find that $\bar{r}_i$ for which $\bar{r}_i \geq \bar{r}_j \forall_j \in \{1, 2, \ldots, m\}$. Bearing this in mind, the proposed procedure is just a straightforward application of this principle.

Because this information is judged to be only partial, an additional measure for the preferability of A_i over the other alternatives is derived by Baas and Kwakernaak (1975).

It cannot be denied that all these procedures look quite complicated and that some scepticism will arise about computational effort. However, Baas and Kwakernaak prove some useful theorems which substantially ease the amount of computational effort.

An analogous evaluation procedure is proposed in Jain (1977). There, exactly the same procedure is adopted for calculating the compositon of fuzzy ratings and fuzzy weights, but the proposal for the final evaluation follows a slightly different line. Starting from the fuzzy weighted rating of alternative $A_i : R_i$, with membership function:

$$\mu_{R_i}(\bar{r}) \qquad\qquad\qquad \text{with } \bar{r} = (\bar{r}_1, \bar{r}_2 \ . \ . \ . \bar{r}_m)$$

the following method is adopted. Form the union S of the support sets of the fuzzy weighted ratings. Now construct the maximising set of set S, $M(S)$, which has a membership function:

$$\mu_M(\bar{r}) = [\bar{r}/\bar{r}_{\max}]^n$$

with:

$$\bar{r}_{\max} = \sup_r S$$

where n is an arbitrary integer. Now for each alternative the intersection is taken between R_i and $M(S)$:

$$\mu_{R_i}(\bar{r}) \wedge \mu_M(\bar{r}).$$

The grade of membership of the alternative A_i in the fuzzy optimal alternative A_* is now defined by:

$$\mu_{A_*}(A_i) = \sup_{\bar{r}} [\mu_{R_i}(\bar{r}) \wedge \mu_M(\bar{r})]$$
$$= \sup_{\bar{r}_1 \ldots \bar{r}_m} [\mu_{R_i}(\bar{r}_1 \ldots \bar{r}_m) \wedge \mu_M(\bar{r}_1 \ldots \bar{r}_m)].$$

Jain (1977) neither explains the reason for adopting this method nor its advantages, and it is difficult to see this procedure as an induction of a fuzzy set by a mapping.

Applications

In Baas and Kwakernaak (1975) the fuzzy multi-criteria problem as set out in Table 6 is tackled with both the fuzzy method and the probabilistic method.

Table 6. The multi-criteria problem.

Criterion	Weight	A_1	A_2	A_3
x_1	Very important	Good	Very good	Fair
x_2	Moderately important	Poor	Poor	Poor
x_3	Moderately important	Poor	Fair to good	Fair
x_4	Rather unimportant	Good	Not clear	Fair

ratings for alternatives (header spanning A_1, A_2, A_3)

A few examples of the fuzzy sets used in this example, which are all defined on the same support set, namely the interval [0, 1], are presented in Figure 10.

This procedure gives the fuzzy weighted alternatives as indicated in Figure 11, and the membership values of the alternatives A_i in the fuzzy set of the best alternative are given in Table 7.

Table 7. The membership function μ_I.

i	$\mu_I(i)$
1	0.95
2	1.0
3	0.77

It will be seen that the second alternative in this table is better than the other alternatives, although not markedly so.

The same problem is also tackled with Kahne's method of random variables. All weights and ratings were taken to be random variables uniformly distributed over the same support sets as the corresponding membership functions. The Monte Carlo method was applied and histograms of the final ratings were computed (Figure 12).

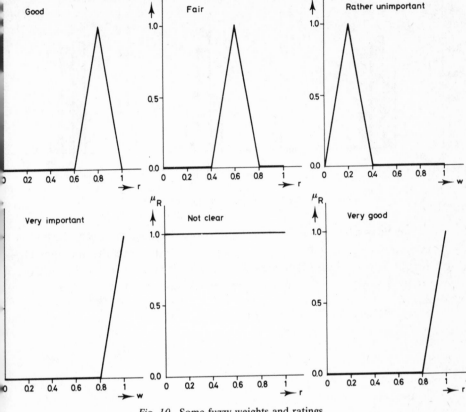

Fig. 10. Some fuzzy weights and ratings.

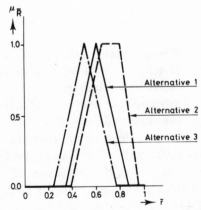

Fig. 11. Membership functions of the final ratings.

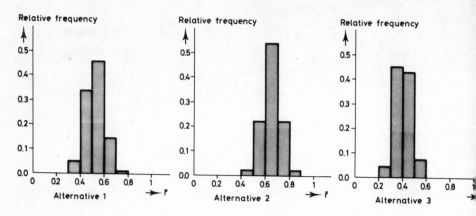

Fig. 12. Histograms of the final ratings.

It may be observed that the density functions decrease rapidly at the higher end, resulting in a bias towards the lower end. Like the membership functions, the density functions show a distinct overlap. Table 8 shows the frequency with which each alternative was ranked first.

Table 8. Frequencies with which the alternatives ranked first.

i	Frequency
1	0.104
2	0.844
3	0.052

From this it is obvious that the probabilistic method results in a much stronger preference for the second alternative.

Both methods are then compared and the following conclusions are reached. The notion of uncertainty is better represented by the fuzzy method than by randomness. One disadvantage of the fuzzy method is that it gives a much fuzzier indication of preferability. On the other hand it does not suffer from the biasing effect and it is well able to carry over uncertainty from prior information to the final rating. Last but not least, the fuzzy method is computationally much easier than the probabilistic method.

Applying their own method to the conclusion, the authors come to a problem formulation as set out in Table 9, which leads to the comparative evaluation of Table 10.

Table 9. Assessment of the relative advantages of Kahne's and the Fuzzy method.

		Ratings	
Aspect	Weight	Kahne's method	Fuzzy method
Appropriateness in representing uncertainty	Important	Fair	Good
Discriminating power	Important	Very good	Fair
Absense of biasing effect	Rather unimportant	Poor	Very good
Propagation of uniform uncertainty	Moderately important	Poor	Very good
Computational effort	Very important	Fair	Good

In Jain (1977) almost exactly the same example is used with regard to the weights, ratings, and fuzzy sets. As mentioned before, the only difference is the method of final evaluation.

Table 10. Comparative evaluation of both methods.

	μ_I
Kahne's method	0.57
Fuzzy method	1.0

4.5. Fuzzy LP and multi-criteria analysis

In this section multi-criteria analysis will be considered from the operations research point of view, namely as linear programming with several objective functions (Zimmermann 1978). This is known as the vector maximum problem. We will first sketch this and then show how fuzzy linear programming (see section 2.4) can be used to single out one specific solution from the set of solutions of the vector maximum problem. It will be shown that in fact this comes down to the choice of a particular aggregation of criteria, namely equal weights and a minimum composition.

The vector maximum problem

The vector maximum problem is defined as:

$$\max \{\underline{z}(x) \,|\, x \in X\}$$

where $\underline{z}(x) = (z_1(x), \ldots z_k(x))$ is a vector valued function of $x \in R^n$ into R^k. $\bar{x}$ is called an efficient solution of the vector maximum problem if $\forall x \in X$:

$$z_i(\bar{x}) \geq z_i(x) \qquad\qquad \forall i \in \{1, \ldots, k\}$$

and:

$$z_i(\bar{x}) > z_i(x) \qquad\qquad \text{for at least one } i \in \{1, \ldots, k\}.$$

The class of all efficient solutions is called the complete solution. In Zimmermann (1978) a linear programming example of the vector-maximum problem is given:

A company manufactures two products 1 and 2 on given capacities. Product 1 yields a profit of 2 units per piece and product 2 of 1 unit per piece. Product 2 can be exported with a profit of 2 units per piece, product 1 needs imported raw material of 1 unit per piece. The two goals are optimal balance of trade and maximum profit. This can be modelled as follows:

$$\max \underline{z}(x) = \begin{pmatrix} -1 & 2 \\ 2 & 1 \end{pmatrix} \begin{pmatrix} x_1 \\ x_2 \end{pmatrix} \qquad \begin{array}{l} \text{balance of trade} \\ \text{profit} \end{array}$$

while the capacity constraints are e.g.:

$$-x_1 + 3x_2 \leq 21$$
$$x_1 + 3x_2 \leq 27$$
$$4x_1 + 3x_2 \leq 45$$
$$3x_1 + x_2 \leq 30$$
$$x_1, x_2 \geq 0.$$

Figure 13 shows the solution space of the problem. The complete solution is the line $x^1 - x^2 - x^3 - x^4$. x^1 is optimal with respect to the first objective $(z_1(x^1) = 14$, maximum net export) while x^4 is optimal with respect to the profit objective $(z_2(x^4) = 21$, maximum profit). Solution x^5 gives the worst results namely $z_1(x^6) = -3$ (3 units imported) and $z_2(x^5) = 7$ (7 units profit). The problem of how to choose one single 'optimal' solution from the complete solution class can be solved by applying the fuzzy linear programming model.

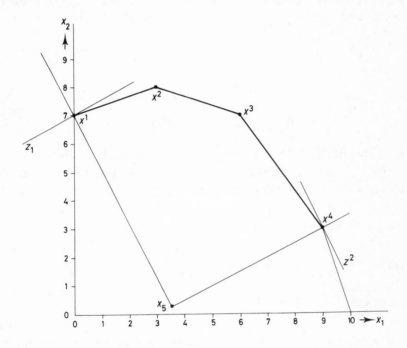

Figure 13. The vector maximum problem.

The corresponding fuzzy linear programme

As has been described in section 2.4 a fuzzy linear programme is a fuzzification of the usual LP problem:

minimise $z = cx$
subject to the constraints $Ax \leq b$ and $x \geq 0$

into a fuzzy version:

$$cx \lesssim z$$
$$Ax \lesssim b$$
$$x \geq 0$$

where the symbol $\lesssim$ denotes 'essentially smaller than or equal to'. This fuzzy inequality is operationalised by taking membership functions $\mu_i (Ax, cx)$ which assume the value zero if the conditions are strongly violated and the value one if the conditions are satisfied. This is translated into linear membership functions of the type:

$$\mu_i((Bx)_i) = \begin{cases} 1 & \text{for } (Bx)_i \leq b_i \\ 1 - \dfrac{(Bx)_i - b_i}{d_i} & \text{for } b_i < (Bx)_i \leq b_i + d_i \\ 0 & \text{for } (Bx)_i > b_i + d_i \end{cases}$$

where B is the matrix formed by adding row c to matrix A, $\mu((Bx)_i)$ is the membership function of the i-th row $(Bx)_i$ of the system Bx, and d_i are constants of admissible violations of the constraints. The fuzzy decision is:

$$\mu(Bx) = \min_i \mu_i((Bx)_i)$$

and the final maximum decision x:

$$\max_x \mu(Bx) = \max_x \min_i \mu_i((Bx)_i).$$

This problem can be shown to be equivalent to a corresponding conventional linear programme, so that it can easily be solved.

This approach can be used to solve the vector-maximum problem. The membership functions for the fuzzy LP problem corresponding to the example become:

$$\mu_1(x) = \begin{cases} 0 & \text{for } z_1(x) \leq -3 \\ \dfrac{z_1(x) + 3}{17} & \text{for } -3 < z_1(x) \leq 14 \\ 1 & \text{for } 14 < z_1(x) \end{cases}$$

$$\mu_2(x) = \begin{cases} 0 & \text{for } z_2(x) \leq 7 \\ \dfrac{z_2(x) - 7}{14} & \text{for } 7 < z_2(x) \leq 21 \\ 1 & \text{for } 21 < z_2(x) \end{cases}$$

because the highest achievable values of the objectives were 14 units net export $(z_1(x) = 14)$ and 21 units profit$(z_2(x) = 21)$ and the lowest values of the objectives were 3 units import $(z_1(x) = -3)$ and 7 units profit $(z_2(x) = 7)$. If we keep the same non-fuzzy capacity constraints the solution which gives the highest degree of 'overall satisfaction' $(\mu = 0.74)$ is $x^0 = (5.03; 7.32)$ yielding an export of $z_1 = 4.58$ and a profit of $z_2 = 17.38$.

Discussion

Essentially the fuzzy approach consists of the following steps: solve the vector maximum problem, find the 'best' and 'worst' solutions, use these solutions as the boundaries of the fuzzy ranges in the corresponding fuzzy LP problem, and solve this fuzzy linear programme.

In Zimmermann (1978) the question is also studied whether the 'maximising' solutions of the fuzzy LP are always efficient solutions of the corresponding vector maximum problem. It turns out that this is indeed always true.

When we try to translate this fuzzy approach into the usual formulation of the multi-criteria problem in terms of criteria and aggregation of criteria we notice the following relationships; the original vector maximum problem is a multi-criteria problem where all objectives (the criteria) are in fact incomparable, that is, there is no way of aggregating the criteria into one overall criterion. By using the fuzzy LP approach implicitly a particular aggregation is chosen, namely equal weighting of criteria and a minimum composition. The equivalent conventional LP problem is namely defined as

$$\max_x \min_i \left[\frac{(b_i - (Bx)_i)}{d_i} \right]$$

where the last rows $(Bx)_i$ are formed by the objectives $z_i(x)$. So we see that the objectives $z_i(x)$ are composed via the minimum operation and that equal weights are attached to them. From the point of view of multi-criteria analysis these implicit assumptions are arbitrary. From the point of view of fuzzy decision theory they stem from the basic assumption that a fuzzy decision is the intersection of fuzzy goals and fuzzy constraints, and that the intersection is usually defined by the minimum operator. Hence in the fuzzy point of view the choice of the aggregation of criteria is shifted to the choice of the definition of the 'and' connective.

In Hamacher (1975) it is shown that if the connective satisfies the following 'rationality axioms':

- it is associative;
- it is continuous;
- it is injective in each argument;
- it is a rational function;
- $\underset{x \in [0,\,1]}{\wedge} D(x, x) = x \iff x = 1$

then the connective D, corresponding to the logical 'and' has to be:

$$D_\gamma(\mu_A, \mu_B) = \frac{\mu_A \mu_B}{\gamma + (1 - \gamma)(\mu_A + \mu_B - \mu_A \mu_B)} \qquad \gamma > 0.$$

If we choose the value $\gamma = 1$ for the arbitrary parameter γ then:

$$D(\mu_A, \mu_B) = \mu_A \cdot \mu_B$$

In Zimmermann (1978) this definition is also adopted to evaluate the fuzzy LP problem corresponding to a vector maximum problem.

In Yager (1977) the multi-criteria problem is similarly presented according to the framework of a fuzzy decision. However the problem of aggregation of criteria is not tackled by studying the intersection but by introducing weighting factors. Consider the following personnel recruitment problem. There are four candidates for a job $-x_1, x_2, x_3$ and x_4 $-$ and three objectives $-$ A, B, and C. The rating of alternative candidate x_i according to objective (criterion) A, B or C can be subjectively evaluated and expressed as a membership value, yielding three fuzzy sets:

$$C_1 = \sum_{i=1}^{4} \mu_A(x_i)/x_i$$

$$C_2 = \sum_{i=1}^{4} \mu_B(x_i)/x_i$$

$$C_3 = \sum_{i=1}^{4} \mu_C(x_i)/x_i.$$

Instead of taking the definition of the fuzzy decision:

$$D = C_1 \cap C_2 \cap C_3$$

and taking that final decision x_i which has the highest membership value, Yager (1977) introduces weighting factors for the importance of the several objectives. Each objective is assigned a number $\alpha \geq 0$ (the more important the higher α) and the decision becomes:

$$D = C_1^{\alpha_1} \cap C_2^{\alpha_2} \cap C_3^{\alpha_3}$$

that is, the intersection of the powers of the fuzzy sets. The numbers α, indicative of the relative importance of the objectives, are obtained via an eigen vector method developed by Saaty (1974).

Remark that the ranking of alternatives according to objectives is the same as presented in the application example in Section 4.2. and hence is subject to the same criticism as mentioned there. Moreover it is obscure why this particular form of weighting by means of powers of fuzzy sets should be adopted, contrary to the usual mutiplicative weighting factors.

4.6. Discussion

Several ways of handling a situation in which a set of alternatives is ranked according to a number of criteria – the situation of multi-objective decision-making – have been outlined in this chapter.

In the first method the introduction of fuzzy sets in this area is done in a mathematically very elegant way by defining a criterion as an L-fuzzy set. However, this procedure seems to have a rather restricted practical relevance in the sense that there is some reasonable doubt on how to obtain the various fuzzy membership values for the ratings.

The second method presented looks rather appealing in terms of practical relevance. This method enables the use of linguistic ratings such as 'good', 'very good', 'fair', etc., and the weights of criteria can be similarly represented by forms such as 'important', 'rather important', etc. The method has been extensively compared with a probabilistic method of evaluating multi-criteria decisions and seems to be preferable both as far as the incorporation of uncertainty is concerned and in the computational effort required. In view of the emphasis on practical applicability throughout this book, this last result is quite reassuring.

The third method also seems to be of practical relevance. In this approach multi-objective decision-making under constraints is modelled as a fuzzy linear programme. Although it has been shown that via the framework of fuzzy decisions some implicit assumptions have been made about the aggregation of criteria which seems rather arbitrary, the method is well-suited to solve practical problems. Moreover serious investigations into the underlying implicit assumptions have been carried out yielding some significant indications on what particular framework to choose. The fact that these mathematical programming studies are performed in a typical OR setting fortunately guarantees a continuing emphasis on the applicability of the developed methods.

Part Two

Multi-stage decision-making

Multi-stage decision-making

In the previous four chapters several fuzzy theories about one-stage deci-sion-making have been presented. In this part we shall describe and discuss some fuzzy theories on multi-stage decision-making.

The importance of the fact that decision-making is essentially a multi-stage process, rather than a one-stage action, has not been fully recognised by mathematical decision theory, if we judge by the relatively small part of the theory that is devoted to it. On the other hand in management science – in some sense the field of application for decision theory – the need for dynamic theories on decision-making has been strongly recognised. The so-called 'decision-making' school in management science has actually concentrated on the dynamic aspect of decision-making. Starting from the fundamental ideas of Simon (1947), through the elaboration in March and Simon (1958), up to the phase-models as proposed in Cyert and March (1963) and more recently in Mintzberg et al. (1976), management science has shown, and is still showing, a deep concern for the dynamic aspects of decision-making. Although we are considering only mathematical decision theories in this book, this interest in management science can at least highlight the practical importance of dynamic decision theories.

Although the importance of the dynamics of decision-making is rela-tively underestimated in mathematical decision theories, there are still quite a lot of theories about multi-stage decision-making. Unfortunately the systematic classification schemes of Part One do not make much sense with these theories.

Take e.g. the classification presented in Part One which used the dimen-sions 'number of stages', 'number of decision-makers', and 'amount of vagueness' (see Figure 1). Bearing this classification in mind one would expect in this chapter some theories which combine multi-stage with multi-person decision-making. This is not the case. Even in non-fuzzy conven-tional decision theories there does not exist a specific theory about multi-person multi-stage decisions. Apart from some dynamisation of game theory (differential games) and some conflict theory which amounts to a system of nonlinear differential equations (Boulding 1962), there are no specific mathematical theories about this subject, so this classification system does not apply.

Of course multi-person multi-stage decision-making might be considered to be covered by the theory of coupled systems, part of dynamic systems theory. In fact all multi-stage decision theories can be viewed as part of dynamic systems theory, since the notion of a dynamic system plays a crucial role in all of them. One might even state that dynamic systems theory is identical with multi-stage decision theory in the sense that most dynamic systems also have some kind of performance or cost function which should be optimised. This is the very definition of a decision theory that we adopted in part one. However, this would also mean that a tremendous amount of literature had to be covered, as almost all fuzzy literature deals with some form of dynamic systems. Clearly some kind of restriction has had to be imposed.

In this book we attach the greatest importance to the applicability of the various fuzzy theories. In view of this one might have some reasonable doubt about the identification of multi-stage decision theory with dynamic systems theory, in particular with control system theory. It does not require much conceptual effort to see the similarity between a decision-maker, decision variables, environmental variables, and the decision procedure on the one hand, and the concept of a controller, control actions, states of the control system, and the optimal control strategy on the other. However, the question arises whether highly sophisticated theories such as e.g. optimal control theory, do not rise too far above real-world decision situations. For it should not be forgotten that the main claim of fuzzy extensions of these theories is that they do take account of precisely these situations.

Without wishing to be identified with that group of researchers who criticise all mathematical theories about social systems, one can imagine the scepticism of the enthusiastic practitioner burdened with an ever- increasing amount of sophisticated and high-brow mathematics when he is confronted with a new mathematical theory – fuzzy set theory – which is superimposed on existing sophisticated theories and which claims to be applicable to realistic decision situations. It then looks as if modern science is only able to adapt existing theories to take account of all kinds of deviations from the ideal, instead of inventing new methods to take account of reality itself. That is why we will not give extensive descriptions of general fuzzy systems theory, fuzzy optimal control theory, fuzzy automata theory etc., although these theories represent a relatively large part of the fuzzy literature.

In this second part of the book we will take the direction opposite to sophistication. We shall strip away all the sophistications of systems theory until we are left with the basic notion of a system: a set of elements (variables) and a set of relationships between these elements. Here we introduce fuzziness. The variables become fuzzy in the sense that they are linguistic, and the relationships become fuzzy since they are based on approximate reasoning. We call this a fuzzy linguistic system.

However, it should be noted that this approach implies that we can no longer talk about a 'decision theory' as defined in the introduction to Part One: 'a theory incorporating some minimisation of a cost function'. The reason why the linguistic system approach is nevertheless called a decision theory and why it is extensively described in this part of the book is the following. Decision theories defined as some cost minimisation are only one part of decision-making models, namely the prescriptive models part. This kind of model prescribes how a decision should be taken. The kind of model which describes how decisions are actually taken is called a descriptive decision-making model. And the familiar prescriptive decision models are not accurate and realistic for highly complex decision processes. In these situations descriptive decision models should offer some relief. In our view the linguistic system approach is a promising method with which to model these complex processes. In Section 7.5 we will discuss this matter more extensively.

Nothwithstanding the previous criticism on sophisticated prescriptive decision theories, this part of the survey would be quite imcomplete without some of them. In our view the most important prescriptive multi-stage decision theory is that of fuzzy dynamic programming (Chapter 5). The main reason for this is that the theory is a straightforward extension into multi-stage processes of the notions of fuzzy constraints, fuzzy goals, and fuzzy decisions, that we met in Chapter 2 on fuzzy mathematical programming. It therefore clearly shows the correspondences between one-stage and multi-stage decision theories. A second reason to present this kind of fuzzy extension of prescriptive decision theories is the aforementioned importance of these theories if we judge by the considerable part of fuzzy literature that they occupy. The next, short, chapter on fuzzy dynamic systems (Chapter 6) is mainly the consequence of this latter consideration.

The fuzzy approach that we shall describe in greater detail is the fuzzy linguistic modelling approach to descriptive decision-making models (Chapter 7). As stated before this approach is based on two fundamentals: linguistic variables (Section 7.2) and approximate reasoning (Section 7.3). In this approach the causal relationship between the elements and the deductive rules does not necessarily have to satisfy the classical (false, true) dichotomy. Deductions and conclusions can be vague. The particular form of vagueness that this approach takes account of is that caused by the impossibility of expressing values numerically. All values are expressed linguistically (verbally). Without claiming that the linguistic representation is the only form of vagueness, or even the most important form, it is certainly a frequent one. It is definitely the form of vagueness most often referred to by fuzzy authors when they want to give an example of fuzziness. example of fuzziness.

Although the reader may miss in this part – apart from the distinction between prescriptive and descriptive theories – the kind of detailed systematic classification possessed by the theories in part one, there is an important line which runs through the theories described, namely the degree of fuzziness incorporated. It is no problem to give a general reason why fuzziness should be incorporated in decision theories. The question about what kind of fuzziness is in fact settled by the use of fuzzy sets. The question about what degree of fuzziness is still open. There are various entries where fuzziness can be introduced, such as the goals, the constraints, and also the variables themselves. The additional aspect introduced in this chapter – systems dynamics – also lends itself to fuzzification. Generally speaking, one should have a clear notion about which essential parts of the decision model take account of fuzziness and which parts are left deterministic.

Although the chapters have been divided according to the three approaches mentioned above, it should not be too difficult to recognise that we start with a theory where fuzziness applies only to goals and constraints. We then proceed with the fuzzification of the variables, and subsequently we fuzzify the systems mapping, while we end with a specification of the form of fuzziness, namely the vagueness of natural language.

5. Fuzzy dynamic programming

5.1. Introduction

The notions of fuzzy constraint, fuzzy goal, and fuzzy decision, which were introduced in the chapter about mathematical programming (Chapter 2), can also be extended to apply to multi-stage decision processes.

Without wishing to repeat everything that was explained in Chapter 2, we briefly recall that the decision problem was there formulated as an 'optimisation under constraints'. This same formulation holds good for dynamic programming. This implies that the basic notions of goals and constraints are still fundamental to the dynamic programming approach. Thus, in this approach, as in fuzzy mathematical programming, fuzziness only enters at the level of the goals and constraints. Apart from these concepts, the remaining constituents of the decision model remain deterministic: that is, the variables (both causes and effects) and the process itself.

5.2. Fuzzy dynamic programming

Essentially the theory consits of the imposition of the framework of a fuzzy decision (the intersection of fuzzy goal and constraint) onto the dynamic programming concept (Bellman and Zadeh 1970). We briefly recall the concept of a fuzzy decision. Let X be a set of alternatives. A fuzzy goal G is then defined as a fuzzy (sub)set on X, and a fuzzy constraint C is likewise defined as a fuzzy (sub)set on X. The fuzzy decision D resulting from the fuzzy goal and fuzzy constraint is defined as the intersection of both: $D = G \cap C$. For a more detailed presentation of the concept of a fuzzy decision we refer the reader to the chapter on fuzzy mathematical programming (Section 2.2). We now arrive at the description of fuzzy dynamic programming. Assume that the process about which decisions have to be made is a time-invariant finite-state deterministic system. The state space is $X = \{x_1 \ldots x_n\}$, the input space is $U = \{u_1 \ldots u_m\}$, and the state transition function is $f : X \times U \to X$. The state equation is

$x_{t+1} = f(x_t, u_t)$, $t = 0, 1, 2 \ldots$ (note that if the system is stochastic the transition becomes a conditional probability). It is assumed that at each instant t the input is subject to a constraint C_t, which is a fuzzy set on U characterised by a membership function $\mu_{C_t}(u_t)$. We suppose a fuzzy goal G_N imposed on the final state x_N characterised by a membership function $\mu_{G_N}(x_N)$. Applying the previously mentioned definition of a fuzzy decision, the decision here is a fuzzy set D on $U \times U \times \ldots \times U$:

$$D = C_0 \cap C_1 \cap \ldots \cap C_{N-1} \cap \overline{G}_N$$

where $\overline{G}_N$ is the fuzzy set on $U \times U \times \ldots \times U$ which induces the fuzzy set G_N on X.

We now recall the definition of an induced fuzzy set: the fuzzy set $\overline{G}$ on X which induces a fuzzy set G on Y, via a mapping $f : X \to Y$ is defined by:

$$\mu_{\overline{G}}(x) = \mu_G(f(x)) = \mu_G(y) \qquad\qquad\qquad y = f(x).$$

This gives the membership function of D:

$$\mu_D(u_0, u_1, \ldots u_{N-1}) = \mu_{C_0}(u_0) \wedge \ldots \wedge \mu_{C_{N-1}}(u_{N-1}) \wedge \mu_{G_N}(x_N)$$

where x_N is a function of $u_0 \ldots u_{N-1}$ via the state equation.

If as a final evaluation procedure on this resulting fuzzy decision we take that decision where the membership function is maximal, we shall choose that $(u'_0 \ldots u'_{N-1}) \in u^N$ for which:

$$\mu_D(u'_0 \ldots u'_{N-1}) = \max_{u0 \ldots uN-1} \mu_D(u_0 \ldots u_{N-1}).$$

One possible way to solve this problem is by using a dynamic programming approach. We apply the principle of optimality and state that:

$$\mu_D(u'_0 \ldots u'_{N-1}) = \max_{u0 \ldots uN-2} \left[\max_{uN-1} \hat{\mu}_{C_0}(u_0) \wedge \ldots \wedge \mu_{C_{N-2}}(u_{N-2}) \wedge \right.$$
$$\left. \mu_{C_{N-1}}(u_{N-1}) \wedge \mu_{G_N}(f(x_{N-1}, u_{N-1})) \right]$$

which can be rewritten as:

$$\max_{u0 \ldots uN-2} \left[\mu_{C_0}(u_0) \wedge \ldots \wedge \mu_{C_{N-2}}(u_{N-2}) \wedge \mu_{G_{N-1}}(x_{N-1}) \right]$$

with:

$$\mu_{G_{N-1}}(x_{N-1}) = \max_{u_{N-1}} \left[\mu_{C_{N-1}}(u_{N-1}) \wedge \mu_{G_N}(x_N) \right].$$

Repeating this backward iteration, we obtain the familiar recurrence equations:

$$\mu_{G_{N-n}}(x_{N-n}) = \max_{u_{N-n}} \left[\mu_{C_{N-n}}(u_{N-n}) \wedge \mu_{G_{N-n+1}}(x_{N-n+1}) \right]$$

with:

$$x_{N-n+1} = f(x_{N-n}, u_{N-n}) \qquad\qquad \text{where } n = 1, 2, \ldots N$$

The decision $u'_0, \ldots, u'_{N-1}$, which maximises the fuzzy decision, is obtained by successively maximising the recurrence equation, resulting in the successive $u'_{N-n}, n = 1, 2 \ldots N$. We take a simple example from Bellman and Zadeh (1970) to illustrate the method.

Consider a system with three states x_1, x_2, x_3 and two inputs u_1 and u_2. Assume a termination time of $N = 2$. Let the fuzzy goal at $t = 2$ be defined by:

$$\mu_{G_2}(x_1) = 0.3; \ \mu_{G_2}(x_2) = 1; \ \mu_{G_2}(x_3) = 0.8$$

and let the fuzzy constraints at $t = 0$ and $t = 1$ be defined by:

$$\mu_{C_0}(u_1) = 0.7; \ \mu_{C_0}(u_2) = 1$$
$$\mu_{C_1}(u_1) = 1 \ \ ; \ \mu_{C_1}(u_2) = 0.6.$$

The state transition table is assumed to be as in Table 11.

Table 11. State transition table.

	x_1	x_2	x_3
u_1	x_1	x_3	x_1
u_2	x_2	x_1	x_3

Then with fuzzy dynamic programming we obtain the fuzzy goal at $t = 1$:

$$\mu_{G_1}(x_1) = 0.6; \; \mu_{G_1}(x_2) = 0.8; \; \mu_{G_1}(x_3) = 0.6.$$

The corresponding maximising decision is set out in Table 12.

Table 12. Optimal decision at $t = 1$.

State at $t = 1$	Action
x_1	u_2
x_2	u_1
x_3	u_1

In the same way we find for $t = 0$

$$\mu_{G_0}(x_1) = 0.8; \; \mu_{G_0}(x_2) = 0.6; \; \mu_{G_0}(x_3) = 0.6$$

with the optimal decision as in Table 13.

Table 13. Optimal decision at $t = 0$.

State at $t = 0$	Action
x_1	u_2
x_2	u_1 or u_2
x_3	u_1 or u_2

Therefore, if the initial state at $t = 0$ is x_1, the maximising decision is to apply action u_2 and then u_1 and the resulting value of μ_{G_2} is 0.8.

Stochastic system

It will be clear that this approach can also be used in cases where the system under control is stochastic. We then replace the state transitions with conditional probabilities:

$$p(x_{t+1}|x_t, u_t)$$

and we regard the fuzzy goal as a fuzzy event (Zadeh 1968), a concept which was presented in chapter 1. The conditional probability of goal G_N then becomes:

$$P(G_N|x_{N-1}, u_{N-1}) = \sum_{x_N} \mu_{G_N}(x_N) \cdot p(x_N|x_{N-1}, u_{N-1}).$$

The recurrence equations for a stochastic system become:

$$\mu_{G_{N-n}}(x_{N-n}) = \max_{u_{N-n}} [\mu_{C_{N-n}}(u_{N-n}) \wedge E\mu_{G_{N-n+1}}(x_{N-n+1})]$$

with:

$$E\mu_{G_{N-n+1}}(x_{N-n+1}) = \sum_{x_{N-n+1}} \mu_{G_{N-n+1}}(x_{N-n+1}) \cdot p(x_{N-n+1}|x_{N-n}, u_{N-n})$$

and $\mu_{G_{N-n+1}}$ defined as before as a backward iteration.

We shall not further elaborate on the stochastic case, mainly because this would lead to a duplication of the description of fuzzy events and fuzzy random variables contained in Chapter 1. An extension of fuzzy dynamic programming into a probabilistic case simply uses these concepts in the same way.

In Bellman and Zadeh (1970) the approach is elaborated for a deterministic system where the termination time is implicitly fixed by the condition that the process stops when the state reaches a pre-specified set of states: the termination set. This problem can be rewritten as a functional equation for which a reverse flow technique is presented. Because this presentation would require quite a lot of explanation and does not shed much additional light on the principles of the approach, we omit it here.

5.3. Fuzzy and non-fuzzy dynamic programming

As in the previous decision theories an interesting question is how this fuzzy dynamic programming technique is related to the conventional non-fuzzy technique. It should be noted that conventional dynamic programming already suffers heavily from the 'dimensionality problem' – that is, for larger and more complex problems the required computational effort becomes tremendously high. The introduction of fuzzy sets mostly increases this drawback.

In Gluss (1973) the fuzzy dynamic programming technique is further extended and compared with conventional techniques. First the technique is extended to deal with continuous variables. The system that is considered is an N-stage control process starting in state x_0 with the usual state transition equation:

$$x_{t+1} = f(x_t, u_{t+1}) \qquad t = 0, \ldots N - 1.$$

For this system fuzzy goals and constraints can be defined. If it is desirable to attain a state x_N 'close to zero', the fuzzy goal G_N may be defined by:

$$\mu_G(x_N) = \exp(-k|x_N|) \qquad k > 0$$

or by:

$$\mu_G(x_N) = \begin{matrix} 1 - |x_N|/d \\ 0 \end{matrix} \qquad \begin{matrix} -d \le x_N \le d \\ \text{otherwise.} \end{matrix}$$

Similarly the fuzzy constraint may be to keep u_t 'close to zero', which might then be realised by the following fuzzy sets:

$$\mu_{C_t}(u_t) = \exp(-m|u_t|) \qquad m > 0$$

or:

$$\mu_{C_t}(u_t) = \exp(-mu_t^2) \qquad m > 0.$$

Gluss (1973) calls this a form of 'terminal control'. If the fuzzy goal G is also defined for the intermediate states $x_t, t = 0, \ldots, N - 1$ resulting in membership functions $\mu_{G_t}(x_t)$, the control is called 'path control' or 'state regulation'. The easiest way to obtain the optimal decision is adopted: choose that action where the final fuzzy membership function is maximal.

Three alternative definitions of a fuzzy decision as the intersection of goals and constraints are examined.

Min-membership

This definition amounts to the usual minimum intersection:

$$\mu_D(x_0 \ldots x_N, u_1 \ldots u_N) = \bigwedge_{t=0}^{N} \mu_{G_t}(x_t) \bigwedge_{t=1}^{N} \mu_{C_t}(u_t).$$

The disadvantage of this definition is that one single low membership value will drag down the whole result. Moreover, this definition is non-interactive. This aspect has been examined in the chapter on fuzzy mathematical programming (chapter 2). The problem comes down to the meaning one should attach to the concept of intersection (see the epilogue of this book).

In order to judge differently the importance of variables, the following membership function is proposed.

Convex membership

$$\mu_D(x_0 \ldots x_N, u_1 \ldots u_N) = \sum_{t=0}^{N} \alpha_t \mu_{G_t}(x_t) + \sum_{t=1}^{N} \beta_t \mu_{C_t}(u_t)$$

where:

$$\sum_{t=0}^{N} \alpha_t + \sum_{t=1}^{N} \beta_t = 1 \qquad\qquad \alpha_t, \beta_t \geq 0 \forall t.$$

Multiplicative membership

A third alternative definition of the fuzzy decision is:

$$\mu_D(x_0 \ldots x_N, u_1 \ldots u_N) = \prod_{t=0}^{N} \mu_{G_t}(x_t) \prod_{t=1}^{N} \mu_{C_t}(u_t).$$

This definition gives equal weights to all goals and constraints and is also subject to a depressing effect from one low membership value. Moreover, as N increases, μ_D will decrease at an exponential rate. This may, however, be quite realistic: the larger N, the more constraints and goals, the more difficult it is to satisfy them all. The advantage of this multiplicative definition is that μ_D is affected by all membership values and not just by the lowest, the latter being the case with the minimum definition.

The dynamic programme that is derived for all three cases differs slightly from the one in Bellman and Zadeh (1970) in the sense that the resulting iteration is not backward but forward. We shall show this difference by following in some detail the derivation for the first case.

Case I

Suppose that from state x_0 action u_1 moves us to state $x_1 = f(x_0, u_1)$; then the remaining $(N-1)$ stage process can be defined by finding:

$$\mu_{N-1}(x_1) = \max_{u_2 \ldots u_N} \min \left[\mu_{G_1}(x_1) \ldots \mu_{G_N}(x_N); \mu_{C_2}(u_2) \ldots \mu_{C_N}(u_N) \right].$$

Using the principle of optimality in this forward version, we obtain:

$$\mu_N(x_0) = \max_{u_1} \min \left[\mu_{G_0}(x_0), \mu_{C_1}(u_1), \mu_{N-1}(x_1) \right].$$

For $n = 2 \ldots N$ this functional equation generally becomes:

$$\mu_n(x) = \max_u \min \left[\mu_{G_{N-n}}(x), \mu_{C_{N-n+1}}(u), \mu_{n-1}(f(x,u)) \right]$$

with

$$\mu_1(x) = \max_u \min \left[\mu_{G_{N-1}}(x), \mu_{C_N}(u), \mu_{G_N}(f(x,u)) \right].$$

This gives a forward iterative solution for $\mu_1(x)$ consecutively up to $\mu_N(x)$.

Case II

The functional equations become:

$$\mu_n(x) = \alpha_{N-n}\mu_{G_{N-n}}(x) + \max_u \left[\beta_{N-n+1}\mu_{C_{N-n+1}}(u) + \mu_{n-1}(f(x,u)) \right]$$

and

$$\mu_1(x) = \alpha_{N-1}\mu_{G_{N-1}}(x) + \max_u \left[\beta_N\mu_{C_N}(u) + \alpha_N\mu_{G_N}(f(x,u)) \right].$$

Case III

In the case of a multiplicative definition of the fuzzy decision the functional equations become:

$$\mu_n(x) = \mu_{G_{N-n}}(x) \cdot \max_u \left[\mu_{G_{N-n+1}}(u) \cdot \mu_{n-1}(f(x,u)) \right]$$

and

$$\mu_1(x) = \mu_{GN-1}(x) \cdot \max_u [\mu_{CN}(u) \cdot \mu_{GN}(f(x, u))].$$

These fuzzy dynamic programming methods are worked out and compared with conventional non-fuzzy problems in a few examples.

Example 1: A fuzzy terminal regulator

Let the state transition equation be:

$$x_{t+1} = ax_t + bu_{t+1} \qquad\qquad a, b > 0$$

and suppose the membership function for the goal is:

$$\mu_{GN}(x_N) = \exp(-k|x_N|) \qquad\qquad k > 1$$

and for the constraint

$$\mu_{C_t}(u_t) = \exp(-|u_t|) \qquad\qquad \text{for all } t.$$

Note that for $t = 0, \dots N-1$ there are no goals. The condition that $k > 1$ shows the necessity of keeping x_N close to zero prior to keeping u_t close to zero.

The iterative equations for this example become

$$\mu_r(x) = \max_u \min[\exp(-|u|); \mu_{r-1}(ax + bu)] \qquad\qquad r > 1$$

and

$$\mu_1(x) = \max_u \min[\exp(-|u|), \exp(-k|ax + bu|)]$$

which give the following solution:

$$\mu_r(x) = \exp(-k_r|x|) \qquad\qquad r = 1, \dots, N$$

and

$$u' = -k_r x$$

where $k_{r+1} = k_r a/(k_r b + 1)$ and $k_0 = k$. By substituting this in the state transition equation, we obtain the optimal policy:

$$(u_1', \ldots, u_N') = (-k_N x_0, \ldots, -k_N x_0)$$

and the final state:
$$x_N = (k_N/k) x_0.$$

This solution is similar to the problem of minimising the cost function:

$$kx_N^2 + b \sum_{t=1}^{N} u_t^2 \qquad\qquad\qquad k > 0$$

for the same transition function. This gives the following optimal solution:

$$u' = -k_r x/a$$
$$k_{r+1} = k_r a^2/(k_r b + 1) \qquad\qquad\qquad k_0 = k.$$

Example 2: A fuzzy state regulator with multiplicative membership

Consider the same state transition function as in the previous example, but assume that the constraints are defined by:

$$\mu_{C_t}(u_t) = \exp(-u_t^2)$$

and the goals by

$$\mu_{G_t}(x_t) = \exp(-mx_t^2) \qquad\qquad\qquad t < N, m > 0$$

and

$$\mu_{G_N}(x_N) = \exp(-kx_N^2) \qquad\qquad\qquad k \geq m.$$

Now define the fuzzy decision in the multiplicative sense. The problem is then to maximise

$$\mu_D(x_0 \ldots x_N, u_1 \ldots u_N) = \exp\{-[\sum_1^N u_t^2 + m \sum_1^{N-1} x_t^2 + kx_N^2]\}$$

which is the equivalent of minimising:

$$C = \sum_1^N u_t^2 + m \sum_1^{N-1} x_t^2 + kx_N^2.$$

Thus this problem is obviously identical to the non-fuzzy state regulator problem of minimising the quadratic cost function C for the same system.

Example 3: A fuzzy state regulator with convex membership

Consider the membership functions

$$\mu_{C_t}(u_t) = 1 - \frac{u_t^2}{B} \quad |u_t| < \sqrt{B}$$
$$0 \quad |u_t| \geq \sqrt{B}$$

$$\mu_{G_t}(x_t) = 1 - \frac{x_t^2}{A} \quad |x_t| < \sqrt{A}$$
$$0 \quad |x_t| \geq \sqrt{A} \qquad t < N$$

$$\mu_{G_N}(x_N) = 1 - \frac{x_N^2}{C} \quad |x_N| < \sqrt{C}$$
$$0 \quad |x_N| \geq \sqrt{C}.$$

If we exclude all policies in which any $\mu_G(x)$ or $\mu_C(u)$ equals zero, the problem is to maximise:

$$\alpha \sum_1^{N-1} (1 - \frac{x_t^2}{A}) + \beta \sum_1^N (1 - \frac{u_t^2}{B}) + \gamma (1 - \frac{x_N^2}{C})$$

or, since $(N - 1) \alpha = N\beta + \gamma = 1$,

$$1 - \frac{\alpha}{A} \sum_1^{N-1} x_t^2 - \frac{\beta}{B} \sum_1^N u_t^2 - \frac{\gamma}{C} x_N^2.$$

This problem formulation is identical to the non-fuzzy state regulator which should minimise the quadratic cost function:

$$C' = \frac{\alpha}{A} \sum_1^{N-1} x_t^2 + \frac{\beta}{B} \sum_1^N u_t^2 + \frac{\gamma}{C} x_N^2$$

for the same system.

As Gluss (1973) remarks, the choice of a particular membership function for the goals and constraints is a subjective matter. Experience will have to show which form is best; and moreover, it will have to show which is best of the three definitions of a fuzzy decision. This leads to the conclusion that, although there is surely a conceptual difference between fuzzy and non-fuzzy modelling, there are some mathematical equivalents in both the fuzzy dynamic programming method and the more familiar 'classical' dynamic programming method. Clearly the equivalents depend strongly on the form of the fuzzy sets and the definition of intersection; but these can be chosen subjectively.

The approach to fuzzy dynamic programming presented so far is certainly not the only possible way to consider this subject. In Chang (1969) a quite different framework was proposed.

A trivial extension of dynamic programming would be simply to replace the state transition costs by fuzzy costs. However, if we choose to evaluate the final fuzzy cost by taking the usual maximum membership value, the method yields exactly the same results as a classical dynamic programme in which all deterministic costs are assumed to be the values at which the fuzzy cost membership functions are maximal. The reason for this is that the operations which are performed on fuzzy sets, such as the addition of fuzzy costs

$$\mu_{A+B}(y) = \max_{(x_1, x_2): x_1 + x_2 = y} [\mu_A(x_1) \wedge \mu_B(x_2)]$$

reach their maximum for y when the constituent fuzzy sets attain their respective maxima. Optimising the sum of fuzzy costs – in the sense of taking maximum membership values – simply comes down to the sum of the 'optimal' constituent costs; the y^* for which:

$$\mu_{A+B}(y^*) = \max_y \mu_{A+B}(y)$$

is $y^* = x_1^* + x_2^*$ where

$$\mu_A(x_1^*) = \max_{x_1} \mu_A(x_1)$$
$$\mu_B(x_2^*) = \max_{x_2} \mu_B(x_2).$$

5.4. Discussion

Although fuzzy dynamic programming should be considered as an extension of fuzzy mathematical programming into multi-stage decision-making, the presentation in this chapter has shown that the approach is a technique for automatic control rather than a model of human decision-making. Because we shall come back to this aspect elsewhere, we shall here restrict ourselves to a consideration of the method itself.

Clearly the method is both a straightforward extension of the ideas about fuzzy constraints, goals, and decisions which were used to design a fuzzy mathematical programme in chapter 2, and a straightforward application of the basic idea behind dynamic programming – the principle of optimality.

Having extended the classical theory, the usual path has been taken by turning round and proving some equivalents between the fuzzy and the classical theory. This has been done by showing in a few examples that both methods can become identical for some particular choices of fuzzy sets and definitions of intersection. However, the equivalence is by no means generally proven; on the contrary, the examples give the impression that a general equivalence does not hold good. The examples given are too simple to give a real indication of the practical applicability of the method. The constantly returning cases where goals and constraints can only be described in vague terms – 'large', 'small', 'important', etc. – are obvious examples of application, but clearly many more real applications should take place.

6. Fuzzy dynamic systems

6.1. Introduction

The decision theory that was considered in the previous chapter was only fuzzy to a restricted degree: only the goals and the constraints were supposed to be defined vaguely, whereas the variables and the system dynamics were supposed to be deterministic, or at most probabilistic. Hence the obvious next step is to fuzzify the system itself. This chapter will begin with an outline of the theory of fuzzy systems based on the familiar description of a system by means of the state transition and output function. After this presentation of a fuzzy system we shall deal briefly with fuzzy automata, which are of course strongly related to the state description of systems. This chapter will conclude with a section on the concept of a fuzzy system mapping, in which we shall try to give an illustrative derivation of this concept.

6.2. State description of fuzzy systems

Assume that we have a system described by its state equations. In the form of difference equations this yields:

$$x_{t+1} = f(x_t, u_t)$$
$$y_t = g(x_t, u_t)$$

where u_t denotes the input, x_t denotes the state, and y_t denotes the output, all measured at time t, with $u_t \in U$, $x_t \in X$ and $y_t \in Y$.
This system is obviously deterministic because it is represented by two mappings f and g from $X \times U$ to X and Y respectively.

A system is called non-deterministic if x_{t+1} and/or y_t are not uniquely determined by x_t and u_t. In this case we obtain sets of values x_{t+1} and y_t with each pair (x_t, u_t). If we denote these subsets of X and Y by X^{t+1} and Y^t, we obtain 'mappings' of the form:

$$X^{t+1} = F(x_t, u_t)$$
$$Y^t = G(x_t, u_t).$$

Furthermore, assuming that these X^{t+1} and Y^t are fuzzy (sub)sets on X and Y respectively, we then have a fuzzy system which is determined by the conditional membership functions

$$\mu_F(x_{t+1}|x_t, u_t)$$
$$\mu_G(y_t|x_t, u_t).$$

If we take the compositional rule of inference to calculate the fuzzy response of the fuzzy system to a fuzzy input, we obtain the following framework.

Given the abovementioned fuzzy system, denoted by its two conditional fuzzy sets F and G, and given a certain fuzzy input U^t and fuzzy state X^t, the next state X^{t+1} and the output Y^t, both fuzzy sets, are defined by:

$$\mu_{X^{t+1}}(x_{t+1}) = \max_{x_t, u_t} \min \left\{ \mu_{X^t}(x_t) ; \mu_{U^t}(u_t) ; \mu_F(x_{t+1}|x_t, u_t) \right\}$$

$$\mu_{Y^t}(y_t) = \max_{x_t, u_t} \min \left\{ \mu_{X^t}(x_t) ; \mu_{U^t}(u_t) ; \mu_G(y_t|x_t, u_t) \right\}$$

or in short notation:

$$\mu_{X^{t+1}} = \underset{x_t}{\vee} \underset{u_t}{\vee} \left\{ \mu_{X^t} \wedge \mu_{U^t} \wedge \mu_F \right\}$$

$$\mu_{Y^t} = \underset{x_t}{\vee} \underset{u_t}{\vee} \left\{ \mu_{X^t} \wedge \mu_{U^t} \wedge \mu_G \right\}.$$

One assumption underlying these formulas is that the input U^t and the state X^t are non-interactive; otherwise we would have to replace:

$$\mu_{X^t}(x_t) \wedge \mu_{U^t}(u_t)$$

by

$$\mu_{X^t \times U^t}(x_t, u_t)$$

in all the equations.

In the preceding derivation we have followed the original definition of a fuzzy system in Zadeh (1969). It is clear that this definition of a fuzzy system was inspired by the analogy of stochastic systems. The conditional membership function and the notion of non-interactiveness correspond to the notions of conditional probability and independence. However, this use of conditional fuzzy sets G and F is not the only way of defining the state transition and output transform. The concept of a fuzzy relationship might also be used. In the last section of this chapter we shall pay somewhat more attention to the form that these fuzzy transforms may take.

For a more extensive description of the concept of a fuzzy system we refer the reader to Zadeh (1969); for an introduction to Zadeh (1965b); and for an example of how to use the concept to describe theories about behaviour modification to Zadeh (1972a). Because the last article describes how the concept might be used rather than giving a factual application and results, we omit the presentation of it here.

It should be noted that the approach to fuzzy systems outlined here is not the only possible approach, and it is certainly not a general one. If looking for generality, one should treat the problem at a much more abstract level. Algebraic approaches to the construction of fuzzy systems can be found in Arbib and Manes (1975) or in the 'Rumanian School' (Negoita and Ralescu 1974, Negoita and Stefanescu 1975).

6.3. Fuzzy automata

The concept of a machine, which is of course strongly related to that of a system in the sense that a machine is a system with finite state, input and output sets, can be fuzzified in the same way. A fuzzy sequential machine FS is an ordered quintuple $FS = \{I, U, Q, f, g\}$ where:

$- I$ is the non-empty finite set of inputs.
$- U$ is the non-empty finite set of outputs.
$- Q$ is the non-empty finite set of states.
$- f$ is the fuzzy set on $Q \times I \times Q$, the fuzzy transition function.
$- g$ is the fuzzy set on $Q \times I \times U$, the fuzzy output transformation.

When $I = \{i_1 \ldots i_p\}$, $U = \{u_1 \ldots u_r\}$, and $Q = \{q_1 \ldots q_s\}$, the fuzzy state transition relation f becomes a p.s.s matrix and the fuzzy output transform relation g becomes a p.s.r matrix.

Just as a sequential machine can be extended to a fuzzy machine, the definition of a finite automaton can be extended to that of a fuzzy automaton. The theory about fuzzy automata is treated in numerous papers, and among the earliest there appeared: theoretical treatments in Santos (1968, 1970), Santos and Wee (1968), and Mizumoto et al. (1969); applications to learning control systems in Wee and Fu (1969) and Asai and Kitajima (1971); and applications to learning pattern recognition programmes in Chang (1971, 1972).

Although we can surely not deny that the theory of fuzzy systems and automata has shown its practical relevance, it will not be examined further in this book. As stated in the introduction to this second part, we do not believe that an extensive treatment of all kinds of sophisticated techniques for automatic control, pattern recognition, and learning systems will shed much light on the applicability of the theories to modelling human decision-making processes. On the other hand, we would not wish to suggest that nothing has been done in this field. For this reason we have restricted ourselves to this very brief presentation.

6.4. Fuzzy system mapping: an illustrative derivation

Rather than discuss the theories on fuzzy systems and automata in greater detail, we shall discuss the underlying general notion, namely the fuzzification of a system's mapping. We shall consider a system mapping in general, without discerning any difference between state transition and output transform mappings. The reason we consider a system mapping so important that we devote a separate section to it is as follows. The basic definition of a system is that a system consists of a set of elements and a set of relationships between these elements. In the familiar system theory this general concept of a system relationship is narrowed down to the concept of a mapping.

We shall try to show step by step how a fuzzy system mapping can be generated, beginning with an ordinary mapping, passing on to an 'ordinary mapping on fuzzy sets' and a 'fuzzy mapping on ordinary sets', and finally dealing with a 'fuzzy mapping on fuzzy sets'.

Ordinary mapping

A mapping F in ordinary set theory is defined as a specific kind of relationship, namely a relationship $F \subset X \times Y$ where one $y \in Y$ is assigned to each $x \in X$ with $(x,y) \in F$ written as $F : X \to Y$ or $F(x) = y$ (figure 14).

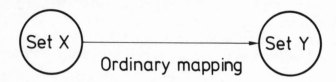

Fig. 14. Ordinary mapping.

This definition of a mapping cannot be extended directly in a fuzzy sense; it is not possible to assign exactly one $y \in Y$ to each $x \in X$ in the case of fuzzy sets. This is inherent in the nature of fuzzy sets.

Ordinary mapping on fuzzy sets

One form of extension could be to define a kind of 'ordinary mapping on fuzzy sets' where the mapping itself remains classical (Figure 15).
Let F be an ordinary mapping from set X to set Y written as $F(x) = y$, $x \in X$ and $y \in Y$. Let $\mu_A(x)$ be the membership function of a fuzzy set A on set X. The mapping F then assigns a fuzzy set B to fuzzy set A in the following way:

$$\mu_B(y) = \max_{x = F^{-1}(y)} \mu_A(x).$$

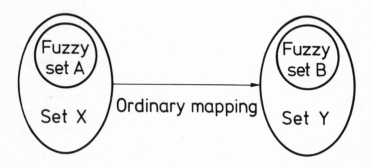

Fig. 15. Ordinary mapping on fuzzy sets.

Clearly this is not a definition of a complete fuzzy mapping.

Fuzzy mapping on ordinary sets

Another form of extension into a fuzzy mapping is to define a 'fuzzy mapping on ordinary sets', this being a fuzzy subset F on the Cartesian product $X \times Y$ with bi-variate membership function $\mu_F(x, y)$ (figure 16). This is identical to the definition of a fuzzy relationship.

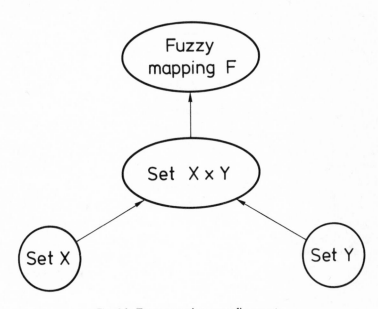

Fig. 16. Fuzzy mapping on ordinary sets.

Fuzzy mapping on fuzzy sets

The next step should then be to define a 'fuzzy mapping on fuzzy sets'. Let the fuzzy set A on X induce a fuzzy set B on Y (Figure 17). Thus the fuzzy set B on Y is the fuzzy mapping of the fuzzy set A on X, and the membership function $\mu_B(y)$ is defined by

$$\mu_B(y) = \mu_{F(A)}(y) = \max_{x \in X} \text{ min } \{\mu_A(x); \mu_F(x,y)\}.$$

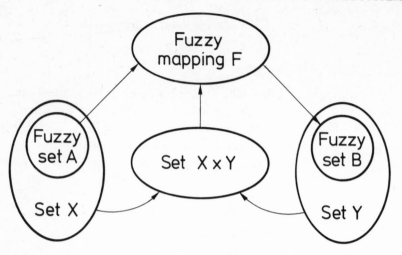

Fig. 17. Fuzzy mapping on fuzzy sets.

This last equation can be interpreted as a definition of a fuzzy system response. While the bi-variate membership function describes the fuzzy system transformation, this formula defines which output will result from a particular fuzzy input.

Although this definition of 'a fuzzy mapping on fuzzy sets' is of course not new, and is indeed the most usual form of a system mapping, we hope to have illustrated the various degrees and levels of fuzziness in the successive definitions of 'fuzzy mappings'. In the next chapter we shall introduce a form of fuzzy relationship where the 'fuzzy mapping F' is itself constructed from the constituent fuzzy sets (Figure 18).'There the 'mapping' is a fuzzy implication of the form: if A then B. This fuzzy implication can then be used to make deductions from other fuzzy statements (Figure 19), so that it can also be regarded as a system response.

6.5. Discussion

Although it looks as if we have lost the connection with decision-making, it should not be forgotten that control systems are models of decision processes. However, the hypothesis that the huge number of methods and

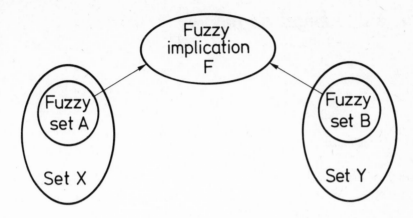

Fig. 18. Fuzzy implication.

Fig. 19. Deductive fuzzy system.

techniques developed for control systems, in other words control theory, is also directly applicable to handling decision processes seems questionable. Therefore, though the derivation of a fuzzy system is certainly useful for modelling decision processes, we have not investigated in detail fuzzy learning automata and optimal control systems and have kept this chapter very short. In our view the usefulness of the derivation of fuzzy systems to decision-making models lies mainly in the feeling one gets about the various levels at which fuzziness can be introduced and the various ways to achieve this. We have tried to illustrate these levels and ways by elaborating on the derivation of the concept of a fuzzy system mapping.

7. Fuzzy linguistic models

7.1. Introduction

In the previous chapter fuzzy systems were discussed in an abstract way. We arrived at a mathematical description of a fuzzy system in terms of state transition and output mapping. It is undeniable that this kind of system description opens up new realms, however these realms have still to be investigated. Though this fuzzy system may appear to cope with inexactness, uncertainty, and fuzziness, at first sight it also seems that the required amount of exact definitions has even increased. Roughly speaking, one actually has to define an extra dimension, namely the truth value space.

As stated in the introduction to Part Two of this book, it seems questionable whether the very sophisticated theories, methods, and techniques thus constructed are directly applicable to handling decision processes as they occur in reality. The applications seem rather to centre around learning theory and optimal control. In this chapter we will present an approach to the modelling of fuzzy systems which is based on a linguistic representation of vagueness. We call this fuzzy linguistic modelling. As stated in the introduction to Part Two this approach starts from the most general definition of a system, namely as a tuple $\langle A, R \rangle$, where A is a set of elements and R is a set of relationships linking the elements of A. Although in engineering literature the state transition description of a system is the most familiar, one should not forget that this definition is much more general because nothing is yet specified about either the elements or about the relationships. Because of its generality this is the definition of a system that is usually adopted in social scientific theories.

According to this basic definition the introduction of fuzziness into a system can be done at the level of the elements (variables) and at the level of the relationships. A fuzzy system consists of fuzzy elements and fuzzy relationships. The particular form of fuzziness that will be treated in this chapter is the linguistic form. Bearing in mind the above-mentioned system definition it will not be difficult to understand that the theory of fuzzy linguistic systems that we will treat in this chapter is composed of a theory of linguistic variables and a theory of fuzzy causal relationships: the theory of approximate reasoning.

As concerns the choice for the linguistic representation of fuzziness – which of course is only one of the possible forms of appearance of vagueness – we can state that this form of vagueness is a very frequently encountered one. All kinds of propositions, statements, relationships: variables etc., are expressed in a natural (or artificial) language. How often do we not meet qualifications like 'high', 'low' and so on instead of exact numerical quantifications? Moreover it will not have passed unnoticed that in almost all the theories discussed in this book the illustrative examples use exactly this kind of vagueness. This form of vagueness seems therefore important enough to be investigated. This has been done in the theory of linguistic variables which has been originated and stimulated over the last few years by Zadeh (1972b, c, 1973, 1975a). This theory will be outlined in Section 7.2.

As concerns the choice for approximate reasoning: in reality it seems to play at least as important a role as the use of linguistic vagueness. Actually if we define approximate reasoning as reasoning with vague statements it is clear that human approximate reasoning is very strongly related to the typical human form of vagueness: the linguistic form. Rather than describe fuzzy linguistic systems with some kind of fuzzified 'systems mapping' or 'transition function' we prefer to fuzzify the concept of implication, to fuzzify the rules of inference, in short to fuzzify reasoning. The theory of fuzzy reasoning that has evolved from this is receiving more and more interest, for example in Zadeh (1975a) and Gaines (1976a, b) and will be presented in Section 7.3.

Because of the importance of both the theory of linguistic variables and the theory of approximate reasoning, both will be discussed in separate sections. Afterwards we will proceed with the application of the theory of linguistic models, first to control systems (Section 7.4) and then to social systems (Section 7.5). Because we think that the understanding of the concept of linguistic modelling is essential to understand the importance of the approach to decision-making processes we will discuss this matter in this last Section only. For it has been remarked already that this linguistic modelling approach no longer satisfies the definition of decision theory that we adopted in Part One. We will show that this has to do with the distinction between prescriptive and descriptive models.

7.2. Linguistic variables

Linguistic variables are variables whose values are not numbers but words or sentences in a natural or artificial language. This concept has clearly been developed as a counterpart to the concept of a numerical variable. We therefore begin with an illustrative example of a linguistic variable which at the same time demonstrates the parallels with the more usual notion of a numerical variable.

Take, for example, the numerical variable 'age'. This variable can assume as a value all discrete numbers between zero and approximately one hundred. Each figure assumed is a numerical value of the variable.

Now take the parallel linguistic variable 'age'. This variable can assume the values: 'young', 'old', 'rather old', 'very young', etc. Each of these terms is a linguistic value of the variable. Just as the numerical values assumed by a variable are bounded – they have to belong to the set of integer numbers, fractions, real numbers, or irrational numbers – we want to put a restriction on the linguistic values that a linguistic variable can assume. We want to define a set of linguistic values to which any possible value should belong in order to be an admissible value of a variable. This set will be called the term-set.

Syntactic definition of a term-set

One possible way of defining such a term-set is by simply enumerating all different terms that should belong to the set. It is clear that this could be a huge and chaotic task. An alternative approach is to define some rules which these values should satisfy. (This is also the way in which integers, fractions, etc. are defined.) In the theory of linguistic variables that has been developed so far this term-set is defined by syntactic rules which generate the possible values; in other words, this term-set is defined as the language of a generative grammar. This is a very elegant definition, because a generative grammar is a mathematical system that contains rules to produce rows of symbols, and is therefore well suited to give a structural description of a set of terms. Before proceeding further with the theory of linguistic variables, we shall briefly describe the theory of formal languages.

Formal languages

The development of the theory of formal languages, in which the work of

Chomsky (1965) has been very important, was meant to be a structural approach to languages. Since every natural language has its structural basis in the form of its grammar, this approach has focused on the development of formal grammars. A grammar should be viewed as a set of rules and procedures which produce a structurally correct language. Although the origin of the theory is evidently linguistic, it has become clear that it is very difficult or even impossible to formalise natural languages by means of formal grammars. Clearly computer languages provided a strong stimulus in the development of this theory.

A generative grammar is defined as an ordered quadruple, $G = \langle V_H, V_E, P, S \rangle$, for which the following holds good:

- V_H is a finite non-empty set. V_H is called the help or non-terminal vocabulary of G. The elements of V_H are called the non-terminal symbols.
- V_E is a finite non-empty set which is called the end or terminal vocabulary of G. The elements of V_E are called the end or terminal symbols.
- V_H and V_E are disjunct, and $V = V_H \cup V_E$ is called the vocabulary of G.
- P is a finite non-empty set of ordered pairs (ϱ, σ), where $P \subset V^* \times V^*$. (V^* is the set of rows of symbols from V.) The elements of P are called the production rules of G and are mostly indicated as $\varrho \to \sigma$.
- S is an element of V_H and is called the start or sentence symbol of G.

The set of possible rows of terminal symbols generated by G is called the formal language generated by G:

$$L(G) = \{w \mid S \xrightarrow{*} w, w \in V_E^*\}.$$

The following example may illustrate these concepts. Take

$$G = \langle \{S\}, \{a, b\}, \{S \to aS, S \to b\}, S \rangle.$$

This grammar will produce the following (rows of) end symbols:

b (apply $S \to b$), ab (apply $S \to aS$ and $S \to b$ consecutively), a^2b (apply $S \to aS$ twice, followed by $S \to b$).

Clearly the formal language of G becomes:

$$L(G) = \{a^n b \mid n \geq 0\}.$$

This definition of a grammar is too wide in the sense that G generates too much. It can be proved that there is no algorithm which can decide for a given G whether or not an arbitrary row $w \in V_E^*$ belongs to $L(G)$. This induced Chomsky to impose restrictions on grammars, resulting in the following hierarchy. A generative grammar $G = \langle V_H, V_E, P, S \rangle$ is of type i with $i = 0, 1, 2,$ or 3 according to which of the following conditions (i) is satisfied:

0 – no restriction. This type is called an unrestricted grammar.
1 – each production rule is of the form
   $\eta_1 A \eta_2 \rightarrow \eta_1 \omega \eta_2$ where $\eta_1, \eta_2 \in V^*$, $A \in V_H$, and $\omega \in V^+$, except the rule $S \rightarrow \varepsilon$ ($V^+ = V / \varepsilon$ and ε is the null row or symbol.) This type is called a context-sensitive grammar.
2 – each production rule is of the form $A \rightarrow \omega$ where $A \in V_H$ and $\omega \in V^*$. This type is called a context-free grammar.
3 – each production rule is of the form $A \rightarrow a$ or $A \rightarrow aB$, where $A, B \in V_H$ and $a \in V_E$. This type is called a regular grammar (because the generated language is a regular set).

Example of term-set

Returning to the definition of the term-set of a linguistic variable, we shall illustrate this structural form of definition by a simple example. Take a context-free grammar $G = \langle V_H, V_E, P, S \rangle$ where the non-terminal symbols V_H are denoted by capital letters, the set of terminal symbols is $V_E = \{young, old, very, not, and, or\}$, and S is the starting symbol. The production rules P are given by:

$$S \rightarrow A \qquad\qquad B \rightarrow \text{not } C$$
$$S \rightarrow S \text{ or } A \qquad\qquad C \rightarrow D$$
$$A \rightarrow B \qquad\qquad C \rightarrow \text{very } C$$
$$A \rightarrow A \text{ and } B \qquad\qquad C \rightarrow E$$
$$B \rightarrow C \qquad\qquad D \rightarrow \text{young}$$
$$E \rightarrow \text{old.}$$

A term-set T which can be generated by this grammar is $T(\text{age}) = \{young, old, young or old, young and old, not young, very young, \ldots, young or (not very young and not very old), \ldots\}$.

Semantics of linguistic variables

As in the case of natural languages, the term-set can be approached from two sides: the procedures and rules that the language should satisfy – the syntax – and the meaning of the words and sentences – semantics. Having defined which rules the language should satisfy, we are now interested in the definition of the meaning – semantics – of the linguistic values of the term set. This is where fuzzy set theory enters, for each linguistic value is defined as a fuzzy set.

In the example of the linguistic variable 'age' the linguistic value 'young' may be defined as a fuzzy set on the universe of discourse of positive integers. Some values of its membership function may be

$$\mu_A(0) \ = \mu_A(5) = \mu_A(10) = \mu_A(15) = \mu_A(20) = 1.0$$
$$\mu_A(25) = 0.9$$
$$\mu_A(30) = 0.8$$
$$\mu_A(35) = 0.6$$
$$\mu_A(40) = 0.3$$
$$\mu_A(45) = 0.1$$
$$\mu_A(50) = \mu_A(55) = \ldots = 0.0$$

or the membership function may be an analytical function such as (Figure 20):

$$\mu_A(x) = (1 + (0.04x)^2)^{-1}.$$

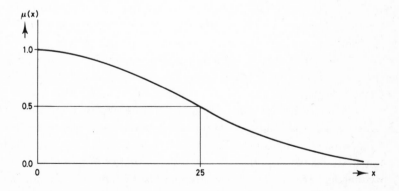

Fig. 20. The fuzzy set representing the linguistic value 'young'.

The inter-relationships between the concepts of linguistic variables, linguistic values, and semantics are illustrated in Figure 21, where 'age' is
again taken as an example (Zadeh 1975a):

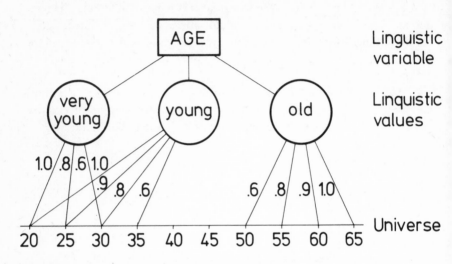

Fig. 21. The linguistic variable 'age'.

As in the case of the syntactic definition of the term-set of a linguistic
variable, it would be a little awkward to define all possible linguistic values
separately as fuzzy sets. Linguistic values such as 'not very old and not
young' or 'more or less old' are obviously composite terms. In the case of
the variable 'age' one might state that we have only two primary terms –
'young' and 'old' – and that all further terms are constructed from these two
by means of connectives such as 'and', 'or', etc., the negation 'not', and the
hedges 'very', 'rather', 'more or less', 'quite', etc. In order to construct the
'meaning' of each linguistic (composite) value of the term-set, we shall
define the primary terms as two fuzzy sets and provide semantic rules M for
the computation of the composite 'meaning' (fuzzy set).

The semantic rule M requires somewhat more explanation. This rule
essentially serves the following purpose: given the meanings of the basic
linguistic values 'young' and 'old', (defined as fuzzy sets), one would like to
be able to derive the meaning of a composite term like X = 'young or (not
very young and not very old)' – in other words, to derive the membership
function of X. This is possible by taking the following semantic rules for the
four connectives:

$$M (A \text{ and } B) = M (A) \wedge M (B),$$
$$M (A \text{ or } B) \; = M (A) \vee M (B),$$
$$M (\text{not } A) \quad = 1 - M (A),$$
$$M (\text{very } A) \quad = (M (A))^2.$$

The computation of the meaning of a composite term is performed by first constructing the syntactic tree of the term, then filling in the meaning of the terminal symbols, and working up the tree to the composite term at the top. The meaning of the example will thus become:

$$M (X) = M (\text{young}) \vee [\{ 1 - (M (\text{young}))^2\} \wedge \{ 1 - (M (\text{old}))^2 \}].$$

There follows a brief presentation of the concept of a linguistic hedge (also discussed in the appendix).*

Linguistic hedges

Zadeh (1972b) gives a rather extensive exposition on linguistic hedges. He proposes considering two types of linguistic hedges:

1. hedges such as 'very', 'more or less', 'quite', etc., which can be represented as operators acting on a fuzzy set.
2. hedges such as 'essentially', 'in a sense', 'strictly', etc., which require a description of how they act on the components of the operand.

The first type of hedges is the most familiar in fuzzy literature. If we take the hedge 'very', the usual definition is:

$$\text{very } x = x^2$$

which means that the membership function of 'very x' is the square of the membership function of 'x':

$$x = \text{old men} = \int_{50}^{100} \left[1 + \left(\frac{y - 50}{5}\right)^{-2}\right]^{-1} / y,$$

---

* Although the term 'hedge' seems rather unclear in view of its meaning – the term 'modifier' would seem to be better, and is used in later publications of Zadeh – we will nevertheless stick to this term because it is widely used and well known.

$$\text{very old men} = \int_{50}^{100} \left[1+\left(\frac{y-50}{5}\right)^{-2}\right]^{-2}\Big/y$$

Other definitions presented by Zadeh (1972) are:

plus $x = x^{1.25}$,
minus $x = x^{0.75}$.

The opposite of the hedge 'very' is 'more or less', so that the definition

more or less $x = x^{0.5}$

is quite evident. Numerous alternative hedges can be thus defined; principally they all come down to the operation

$$f(x) = x^\alpha$$

were α is some real value.

A rather different operator would be one which does not act on the membership function but on the support set of the fuzzy set. One example of such a definition of a linguistic hedge might be:

recent $= 1/1977 + 0.9/1976 + 0.7/1975$
more or less recent $= 1/1976 + 0.9/1975 + 0.7/1974$

where the support has simply been shifted by one year. Of course many alternative operations are possible.

The second type of linguistic hedges applies to a composite linguistic term. This will be illustrated by means of an example taken from Zadeh (1972b). Consider the hedge 'essentially' and assume that its operand is a term x whose components are $x_1 \ldots x_n$. For example $x =$ decent, with the components $x_1 =$ kind, $x_2 =$ honest, $x_3 =$ polite, and $x_4 =$ attractive. Assume that the fuzzy set 'decent' is a convex combination of its components:

$$\mu_x = w_1\mu_{x_1} + w_2\mu_{x_2} + w_3\mu_{x_3} + w_4\mu_{x_4}$$

where w_i, $i = 1, \ldots, 4$ are non-negative weights adding up to unity. The support set of the fuzzy sets is a set of individuals. Take, for example,

$w_1 = 0.4$, $w_2 = 0.3$, $w_3 = 0.2$, and $w_4 = 0.1$. Then if $\mu_1(\text{John}) = 0.9$, $\mu_2(\text{John}) = 0.8$, $\mu_3(\text{John}) = 0.9$, and $\mu_4(\text{John}) = 0.2$, we have

$$\mu_{\text{decent}}(\text{John}) = 0.4 \times 0.9 + 0.3 \times 0.8 + 0.2 \times 0.9 + 0.1 \times 0.2 = 0.8.$$

The hedge 'essentially' can now be interpreted as increasing the weights w_i of important components and diminishing the weights of those that are relatively unimportant. This can be achieved by the following procedure:

– normalise the weights, $w'_i = w_i / \max_i w_i$.

– form the weights, $w^*_i = (w'_i)^2 / \sum_i w'_i$.

– adopt w^*_i as the weights of 'essentially decent'.

Of course, any form of contrast intensification would do, such as:

$$w^*_i = 2w^2_i \qquad \text{for } 0 \leq w_i \leq 0.5$$
$$w^*_i = 1 - 2(1 - w_i)^2 \quad \text{for } 0.5 \leq w_i \leq 1.$$

The essence of this second type of linguistic hedges might also be attained by using operators on the membership functions or support sets of the fuzzy components, as in the first type of hedge.

We shall now continue by presenting the formal definition of the concept of a linguistic variable (Zadeh 1975a).

Definition of a linguistic variable

A linguistic variable is defined by a quintuple $\{A, T(A), U, G, M\}$ in which A is the name of the linguistic variable, $T(A)$ is the term-set of A, that is, the set of names of linguistic values that A can assume where each linguistic value of A, denoted by X, is a fuzzy set on the universe of discourse U. G is a syntactic rule (usually a generative grammar) for generating the names of the values of A, that is, for generating the term-set $T(A)$. M is a semantic rule for assigning the meaning $M(X)$, which is a fuzzy sub-set on U, to each X from $T(A)$. A particular name for a linguistic value, X, is called a term. For a thorough treatment of the theory of linguistic variables we refer the reader to Zadeh (1975a).

7.3. Fuzzy logic and approximate reasoning

In this section we shall describe a fuzzy set theory approach to human reasoning. The starting-point for this approach is – as usual – the extension of classical formal models of reasoning into models that incorporate fuzziness. Because it is widely felt that the framework of formal logic is not particularly suitable for imprecise real-world problems, there have consequently been many extensions and alterations to the most classical form of formal logic, the propositional calculus. The rejection of the opinion that human reasoning could be specified and refined to fit exact formal logic, and the assumption that the power of human reasoning contrarily lies in its ability to handle inexact concepts directly, led Zadeh to introduce his concept of a fuzzy set in 1965. Since then, and particularly in the last few years, Zadeh has concentrated on the construction of a framework for fuzzy reasoning, usually called fuzzy logic, which, incidentally, is something more than just that theory of fuzzy sets (Zadeh 1973 and 1975b). As a simple illustration of what is meant by fuzzy reasoning, compared with formal reasoning, consider the following two examples:

> Socrates is a man
> All men are mortal
> ∴   Socrates is mortal

and

> Socrates is *very healthy*
> *Healthy* men live *a long time*
> ∴   Socrates will live *a very long time*.

Obviously in the second example the italicised words are imprecise concepts; in fuzzy logic these are represented by fuzzy sets.

Compositional rule of inference

Another example of fuzzy reasoning which leads to the basic concept behind this theory is:

> x is small
> x and y are *approximately equal*
> ∴ y is *more or less small*.

The concept which supports this form of fuzzy reasoning is the compositional rule of inference: given a relationship R and an implicand A, the implied result is $B = A \circ R$, where o denotes the usual composition of fuzzy relationships.

Although a numerical example rather confuses the essentially non-numerical linguistic basis of this type of reasoning, we hope that the illustrative advantage outweighs this drawbak. Suppose that we take the following definitions:

$$\text{small} = 1/1 + 0.6/2 + 0.2/3$$

and

$$\text{approximately equal} = 1/[(1,1) + (2,2) + (3,3) + (4,4)] +$$
$$+ 0.5/[(1,2) + (2,1) + (2,3) + (3,2) + (3,4) + (4,3)].$$

The implied result is then:

$$y = 1/1 + 0.6/2 + 0.5/3 + 0.2/4$$

which can be approximated by the linguistic value

$$y \cong \text{more or less small.}$$

In general, the compositional rule of inference states that:

Given two universes of discourse X and Y, let A be a fuzzy set on X and R a fuzzy relationship on $X \times Y$, characterised by $\mu_A(x)$ and $\mu_R(x, y)$, respectively. The compositional rule of inference states that the result will be a fuzzy set B on Y defined by:

$$\mu_B(y) = \max_x [\mu_A(x) \wedge \mu_R(x, y)]$$

and written as:

$$B = A \circ R.$$

Note that the fuzzy sets A and R are linguistic values of linguistic variables. However, the resulting fuzzy set B will not generally coincide with an element of the set of possible linguistic values (term-set). In order to assign an admissible linguistic value to that fuzzy set we shall have to make a so-called linguistic approximation, that is, assign to B that linguistic value which is closest to it.

Fuzzy implication

So far we have only considered the rule for drawing conclusions from chains of inference. In order to be able to speak of fuzzy logic there is obviously a very important concept that has to be added, namely the concept of implication:

if A then B,

denoted as:

$$A \Longrightarrow B.$$

In his original presentation of fuzzy implication (1973) Zadeh proposes to define 'if A then B' as a special case of the fuzzy implication 'if A then B else C', which he defines as

if A then B else $C = (A \times B) \vee (\neg A \times C)$,

that is, the union of the Cartesian product of A and B and the Cartesian product of $\neg A$ and C.

Remember that the Cartesian product of two fuzzy sets is defined as the minimum of both:

$$\mu_{A \times B}(x, y) = \min [\mu_A(x); \mu_B(y)].$$

Now 'if A then B' is a special case where C is allowed to be the entire universe Y: This is interpreted to mean that Y is a degenerated fuzzy set with all membership values equal to one.

A numerical example of these definitions is the following from Zadeh (1975a). Assume $X = Y = \{1, 2, 3\}$ and

$A = \text{small} \quad = 1/1 + 0.4/2$
$B = \text{large} \quad = 0.4/2 + 1/3$
$C = \text{not large} = 1/1 + 0.6/2$

then

$$\text{if } A \text{ then } B \text{ else } C = \begin{bmatrix} 0 & 0.4 & 1 \\ 0.6 & 0.6 & 0.4 \\ 1 & 0.6 & 0 \end{bmatrix}$$

and

$$\text{if } A \text{ then } B = \begin{bmatrix} 0 & 0.4 & 1 \\ 0.6 & 0.6 & 0.6 \\ 1 & 1 & 1 \end{bmatrix}$$

An alternative definition of $A \Longrightarrow B$ can be derived from 'if A then B else C' by making C equal to the empty set $\emptyset$:

if A then $B = A \times B$.

Fuzzy modus ponens

When we combine the concept of fuzzy implication with that of the compositional rule of inference, we get:

$$\begin{array}{ll} A_1 & \text{implicand} \\ A \Longrightarrow B & \text{implication} \\ \therefore A_1 o(A \Longrightarrow B) & \text{conclusion} \end{array}$$

In fuzzy logic this is the equivalent of the *modus ponens* in formal logic. There is, however, one important difference in this fuzzy *modus ponens*, namely that the implicand A_1 need not be identical to A. It is easily checked that, if A_1 and A are equal and both are non-fuzzy sets, we get:

$$A o(A \Longrightarrow B) = B,$$

which agrees with the conclusion from classical *modus ponens*. If, on the other hand, A_1 and A are equal but remain fuzzy sets, the definition of $A \Longrightarrow B$ as:

$$A \Longrightarrow B = (A \times B) \vee (\neg A \times Y)$$

gives:

$$A \circ (A \Longrightarrow B) = B \vee A \circ (\neg A \times Y) \neq B$$

contrary to classical *modus ponens*. If we assume the definition of $A \Longrightarrow B$ to be:

$$A \Longrightarrow B = (A \times B)$$

then the result agrees with classical *modus ponens*:

$$A \circ (A \Longrightarrow B) = B$$

as long as A is a normal fuzzy set.

Alternative definitions

The reader will have noticed that the abovementioned definitions look rather arbitrary. Apparently there is neither an axiomatic nor another strict derivation for these particular definitions. This implies that other definitions could also be proposed.

However, it is natural that we should impose restrictions on the definitions of implication and compositional inference, restrictions which correspond to the intuitive meanings of both. This intuitive condition that both definitions should satisfy is that the strength of the inferred consequence $A * (A \Longrightarrow B)$ should not exceed the strength of B; in other words:

$$\mu_A * \mu_{A \Longrightarrow B} \leq \mu_B.$$

Moreover one would like the strength of the inference to be as great as possible.

It can be easily verified that the previously adopted definitions of implication $(A \Longrightarrow B)$ and the compositional rule of inference $(*)$ satisfy this condition. However, the following combinations of definitions also satisfy the condition:

$$\mu_{A \Longrightarrow B} = \max [1 - \mu_A; \mu_B]$$

with the minimum operator for $*$ (Lee 1972), or:

$$\mu_{A \Rightarrow B} = \begin{cases} \mu_B/\mu_A & \text{if } \mu_A \geq \mu_B \\ 1 & \text{otherwise} \end{cases}$$

with multiplication for $*$ (Goguen 1969).

Foundations of fuzzy reasoning

These questions on how to define the basic concepts of fuzzy reasoning – fuzzy implication, for example – should not be underestimated. They are the very fundamentals of the whole approach. In fact, the problem can be stated more generally as: what particular forms should the logical operations:

$$\neg A$$
$$A \vee B$$
$$A \wedge B$$
$$A \Rightarrow B$$
$$A \Leftrightarrow B$$

have in fuzzy logic?

The first attempt to give an axiomatic derivation of such particular forms was made by Bellman and Giertz (1973) where they restricted themselves to conjunction and disjunction. They proved that the operators $\wedge$ and $\vee$, being binary operators on the closed interval [0, 1], when they satisfy the following assumptions:

1. $x \wedge y = y \wedge x$, $x \vee y = y \vee x$.
2. $(x \wedge y) \wedge z = x \wedge (y \wedge z)$, $(x \vee y) \vee z = x \vee (y \vee z)$.
3. $x \wedge (y \vee z) = (x \wedge y) \vee (x \wedge z)$ $x \vee (y \wedge z) = (x \vee y) \wedge (x \vee z)$.
4. $x \wedge y$ and $x \vee y$ are continuous and non-decreasing in x.
5. $x \wedge x$ and $x \vee x$ are strictly increasing in x.
6. $x \wedge y \leq \min[x, y]$ and $x \vee y \geq \max[x, y]$
7. $1 \wedge 1 = 1$ and $0 \vee 0 = 0$

can only be of the form:

$$x \wedge y = \min[x, y]$$
$$x \vee y = \max[x, y].$$

This result has been generalised by Hamacher (1975). In these studies the analytic formalism was restricted to ∧ and ∨ and no connection was made with fuzzy logic as a whole.

The investigations into the logical foundations of fuzzy reasoning have been conducted mainly by Gaines (1975, 1976a, 1976b), who has pointed out the relationship between fuzzy logic and other logics of uncertainty such as many-valued logic (MVL). Gaines remarks that first of all it should be clear what is meant by 'fuzzy logic'. In his view there are at least three possible definitions:

1. 'a basis for reasoning with vague statements,' which is a very general definition.
2. 'a basis for reasoning with vague statements using fuzzy set theory for the fuzzification of logical structures,' which is a restricted form of the first definition and comes closest to the contents of Zadeh's papers.
3. 'a multi-valued logic in which truth values are in the interval [0, 1], and the valuation of a disjunction is the maximum of those of the disjuncts, and that of a conjunction is the minimum of those of the conjuncts', which is the form that is widely used.

Gaines notes that the third definition applies to most MVL's that have been studied (Rescher 1969). He describes extensively the properties that 'fuzzy logics' in terms of the third definition should possess in order to be used as a basis for fuzzy reasoning in terms of the other two definitions. The 'fuzzy logic' of definition three can be regarded as a set of infinitely valued MVL's differing only in their implication functions.

In Gaines (1976a) a whole series of MVL's is investigated and characterised according to the underlying properties desired. For example, if we require that the truth value of the implication $A \Longrightarrow B$ is 1, when the truth value of B is greater than or equal to the truth value of A, in other words

$$p(A \Longrightarrow B) = 1 \qquad\qquad \text{if } p(B) \geq p(A),$$

we are left with the definition of $p(A \Rightarrow B)$ for $p(B) < p(A)$. Three possible definitions are:

1. $p(A \Longrightarrow B) = 1$ if $p(B) \geq p(A)$,
   $\quad = p(B)$ otherwise.

2. $p(A \Longrightarrow B) = 1$ if $p(B) \geq p(A)$,
$\qquad = p(B)/p(A)$ otherwise $(0/0 \triangleq 1)$.
3. $p(A \Longrightarrow B) = 1$ if $p(B) \geq p(A)$,
$\qquad = 1 - p(A) + p(B)$ otherwise.

If these definitions are coupled to the definitions:

$$p(A \vee B) = \max[p(A); p(B)]$$
$$p(A \wedge B) = \min[p(A); p(B)]$$
$$p(\neg A) = p(A \Longrightarrow F) \qquad\qquad F \text{ is a false proposition}$$
$$p(A \Longleftrightarrow B) = p((A \Longrightarrow B) \wedge (B \Longrightarrow A))$$

in the first case this gives an infinitely valued logic in which negation has the form:

$$p(\neg A) = 1 \quad \text{unless} \quad p(A) = 1$$
$$\quad\quad = 0 \quad\quad \text{if} \quad\quad p(A) = 1.$$

The second case gives a different MVL with the same form of negation, while the third gives Lukasiewicz's infinitely valued logic with a negation of the form:

$$p(\neg A) = 1 - p(A).$$

Another example of how the particular basic requirements that one demands of the logical system result in different final definitions is shown by Gaines (1975). Here he derives a probability logic which should satisfy

$$p(\overline{A}) = 1 - p(A)$$
$$p(A) = p(A \wedge B) + p(A \wedge \overline{B})$$
$$p(B) = p(A \wedge B) + p(\overline{A} \wedge B).$$

Given the fact that the probabilities lie in the interval [0, 1], the following inequalities are derived:

$$0 \leq p(A \wedge B) \leq \min[p(A); p(B)]$$
$$0 \leq p(A) \cdot p(B) \leq \min[p(A); p(B)]$$
$$\max[p(A); p(B)] \leq p(A \vee B) \leq 1$$
$$\max[p(A); p(B)] \leq p(A) + p(B) - p(A) \cdot p(B) \leq 1.$$

The conditions under which the three values in these inequalities are attained are then considered (Table 14).

Table 14. Fuzzy and Stochastic logic.

$C = A$ and B $p(C) = p(A \wedge B)$	$C = A$ or B $p(C) = p(A \vee B)$
$p(C) = 0 \Longleftrightarrow p(A \wedge B) = 0$ $A \supset \bar{B}$ and $B \supset \bar{A}$, that is, A and B are mutually exclusive.	$p(C) = 1 \Longleftrightarrow p(A \vee B) = 1$ $\bar{A} \supset B$ and $B \supset \bar{A}$, that is, either A or B must occur.
$p(C) = p(A) \cdot p(B)$, that is, A and B are statistically independent.	$p(C) = p(A) + p(B) - p(A) \cdot p(B)$, that is, A and B are statistically independent.
$p(C) = \min[p(A); p(B)] \Longleftrightarrow$ $p(A \wedge \bar{B}) = 0$ or $p(\bar{A} \wedge B) = 0$, that is, the existence of either A or B strictly implies the other.	$p(C) = \max[p(A); p(B)] \Longleftrightarrow$ $p(A \wedge \bar{B}) = 0$ or $p(\bar{A} \wedge B) = 0$, that is, the existence of either A or B strictly implies the other.

This shows that the second case, which is stochastic logic, as well as the third case, which is fuzzy logic, can be viewed as arising from constraints on an underlying probability logic.

The most important conclusion that can be drawn from the investigations into the foundations of fuzzy reasoning is that there is no one logical system that can claim to be the logic of uncertainty (Gaines 1976a). Depending on one's requirements, one or the other logical system will appear suitable. Hence it is not surprising that many applied studies use different logics for different situations in reality.

7.4. Fuzzy logic control

There exist two kinds of practical application of this linguistic modelling concept – in process control (Mamdani 1975 and 1976, Mamdani and Assilian 1975, Kickert and Van Nauta Lemke 1976) and in social science (Wenstøp 1976, Kickert 1976). In this section we shall describe the control application of the linguistic approach.

The reason that we describe this type of fuzzy controller, in spite of our earlier remarks about the dubious usefulness of control system techniques for decision-making theory, lies in the rationale of this particular type of controller. Here fuzzy logic is used to convert heuristic control rules, as stated by a human operator, into an automatic control strategy (Mamdani and Assilian 1975). As Kickert and Van Nauta Lemke (1976) remarked complex industrial processes such as chemical reactions are often difficult to control automatically, and in many cases the control of a process by a human operator is far more successful than any automatic control. Thus it seems worthwhile to investigate the control strategy of the operator. In this sense the fuzzy logic controller is nothing more than a linguistic model of the human operator strategy and is, as such, a decision model.

The operator may be able to express his strategy as a set of linguistic rules in the form: if 'increase in temperature is big' then 'decrease pressure a lot'; alternatively, if 'increase in temperature is low' then 'decrease pressure a little', and so on. Obviously these rules can be translated into fuzzy implications of the form 'if A then B', which were described in the previous section. So the human control strategy, once it is expressed as a set of rules, can be converted into an algorithm in the following way. Assume the definition of an implication as

S : if A then B

$\mu_S(y, x) = \min [\mu_A(x); \mu_B(y)]$

and the definition of the composition rule of inference:

$\mu_{B'}(y) = \max_x \min [\mu_{A'}(x); \mu_S(y, x)]$

as mentioned previously. Naturally, the system cannot be described by just one relationship, but only by a set of fuzzy implications. The final system is considered to behave as the union of all these casual relationships:

S: if A_1, then B_1, or, if A_2 then $B_2 \ldots$ if A_n then B_n

defined by:

$\mu_S(y, x) = \max_i \min [\mu_{A_i}(x); \mu_{B_i}(y)] \qquad\qquad i = 1, 2, \ldots, n.$

In control situations the input has been considered to be precise, namely a measured value (for example, temperature). Therefore, the input can now be considered as a degenerated fuzzy input set A' with

$$\mu_{A'}(x) = 1 \quad \text{if} \quad x = x_0$$
$$= 0 \quad \text{elsewhere}$$

which gives a reduction of the compositional rule of inference:

$$\mu_{B'}(y) = \max_x \min [\mu_{A'}(x); \mu_S(y, x)] = \mu_S(y, x_0).$$

However, not only was the input a non-fuzzy precise value, the output of the controller also had to be an exact value (for example, a valve position). This is solved by applying an evaluation procedure to the final fuzzy output sets to determine which particular output should be considered as the representative of that fuzzy set. A procedure is adopted in which that value y_0 (or the mean of those values) at which the membership function is maximal is taken as the deterministic output of the controller:

$$y_0 \text{ at which } \mu_{B'}(y_0) = \max_y \mu_{B'}(y).$$

Therefore, the final overall procedure can be described as: take that output y_0 for which:

$$\mu_{B'}(y_0) = \max_y \max_i \min [\mu_{A_i}(x_0); \mu_{B_i}(y)] \qquad i = 1, 2 \ldots n.$$

The several steps of the fuzzy logic control algorithn are illustrated in Figure 22.

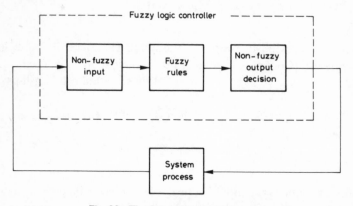

Fig. 22. The fuzzy logic control system.

This framework was originally proposed in Mamdani (1975) and Mamdani and Assilian (1975), where the controller was applied to a small steam engine. Since then numerous other applications have been published, recent surveys of fuzzy logic control being Mamdani (1976) and Tong (1977).

Undoubtedly the practical applicability of this fuzzy logic control method is high. The first application achieved a good control of a time-variant and non-linear coupled system: the small steam engine in Mamdani and Assilian (1975). Fuzzy control of a warm-water plant resulted in a faster and more accurate control than conventional control techniques (Kickert and Van Nauta Lemke 1976 and Van Nauta Lemke and Kickert 1976). Other applications that have been performed separately are the control of a strongly coupled, two-input, two-output system; the control of an industrial sinter-making plant at the British Steel Corporation (see the survey of Mamdani 1976); and the control of a pilot-scale batch chemical process with large time-lags and non-linearities (King and Mamdani 1975, Kickert 1975). Thus there is certainly no lack of applications. Moreover there exist some attempts at an analysis of fuzzy logic control such as those of Kickert and Mamdani (1978); and Tong (1976).

From the point of view of decision-making models a very important aspect of the method, namely the derivation of the control rules from the human operator, has proved to be rather troublesome. In industrial psychology it is well-known that a great deal of effort is required to derive the control protocol from the human operator (Bainbridge 1975). Until now most of the fuzzy logic controllers have contained a set of rules obtained by the researcher and for the greater part based on common sense. Although these controllers have performed very well, this poses some questions about the original intention that the algorithm should be a translation of a successful operator's strategy. In other words, though the very successful performance means that this method is certainly suitable as a prescriptive decision-making model, so far there is no proof that it is also suitable as a descriptive decision-making model. For the time being we have to be content that this translation of a decision strategy into an algorithm is at least quite appealing.

7.5. Linguistic models in social sciences

Although one could imagine that the intrinsically vague and imprecise approach of linguistic modelling had be better applied to the so-called 'soft sciences' rather than to 'hard sciences' (like control theory), it was only very recently that an application study appeared where the method had been used to model organisational behaviour (Wenstøp 1976). A similar approach has been used to model a social-psychological theory about power relationships (Kickert 1976).

In these approaches the linguistic model is used as a simulation model. As in the case of the fuzzy logic controllers, the linguistic model is a translation of a set of verbal relationships into a fuzzy algorithm. In these approaches the verbal relationships were derived from the social scientific theories that were modelled.

Prescriptive and descriptive models of decision-making

Before actually passing on to the presentation of the linguistic simulation models, we shall try to justify the importance of these models to decision-making, for the reader will have noticed that the definition of a decision theory as 'a theory incorporating some minimisation of a cost function' no longer applies to these models.

A fundamental division of decision-making models is that into prescriptive (normative) models and descriptive models. In the first case one is concerned with the question of how people should take decisions rationally, whereas the second is concerned with the question of how people actually take decisions.* Apparently, the essence of prescriptive decision-making models is the concept of rationality. Although whole libraries could be filled with discussions about this concept, it is usually understood to mean that rational behaviour is goal-orientated behaviour (Simon 1947, ch. IV). This is the origin of our definition of a decision-making theory in the first part of this book, for viewed mathematically goal-attainment can be represented by the optimisation of a value (minimisation of costs or maximisation of utility). However, actual decision-making often does not take place in a rational way, and it is impossible for decision-making always to be mathematically modelled as an optimisation. So long as we are taking one single decision-maker and not looking at dynamic aspects, things may still work; as soon as the number of decision-makers increases, as decision-making becomes a dynamic process – in short, as soon as decision-making becomes a complex process – the familiar prescriptive mathematical models fail. This

---

* Methodologists will argue that all theories and models are normative. This is related to the impossibility of objectivity in perception, so that ultimately every observer somewhere introduces his own values.

is where descriptive models should at least be investigated before anything prescriptive can be said.

Descriptive models describe how people actually take decisions. Clearly these kinds of models are not constructed with concepts of goals, constraints, and optimality in mind. Descriptive models have to meet other criteria, namely the criteria for a 'good' description. A 'good' descriptive model of some real system should be a mapping of the variables and relationships in that system. In mathematical models these mappings of the system's relationships are usually mappings themselves. Of course this is surely not the only possible representation for in most social scientific models the relationships are at best represented by verbal statements. It is this latter type of descriptive model which will be treated in this section by means of the linguistic modelling approach.

The class of descriptive models itself can further be sub-divided into analytical and non-analytical models. Some models can be analysed in a mathematical way and others cannot. Especially highly complex models can often not be analysed. In this case we can use the technique of computer simulation, that is, one simply runs the model on a computer to see what happens.

The linguistic models that are discussed in this section are computer simulation models. Besides the complexity of the modelled systems the simple reason for this is that, as opposed to the usual models in terms of linear differential (or difference) equations, suitable tools for the analysis of the linguistic type of model itself do not yet exist.

Simulation and decision-making

It has been shown that the technique which is pre-eminently suited to the descriptive modelling of complex systems is the technique of computer simulation. It is therefore not surprising that this technique is well-known in the social sciences. In the area of organisational decision-making several simulation models have been proposed to explain and predict organisational decision-making behaviour (Cyert et al. 1959, Cohen and Cyert 1965, Cyert and March 1963, Cohen et al. 1972).

In the area of individual decision-making the information processing analysis of human problem-solving is well known to be based on computer simulations (Newell and Simon 1972).

An introduction to the problems of computer simulation in the social sciences is given in Harbordt (1974). This gives, for example, a summary of the advantages of computer simulation models, a few being:

– the use of a formalised language forces a theorist to express himself clearly and precisely.
– the logical structure between the concept and the propositions has to be made clear.
– they enable us to discover gaps in our knowledge.
– the system of propositions can be tested empirically without the use of re-interpretation and *ad hoc* explanations to save the model or theory from falsification.
– they permit fast, correct deductions from complex systems of proposi-tions that are not disturbed by or adapted to wishful thinking.
– they show how processes progress in time; they dynamise a theory.
– they make it easy to use large amounts of data effectively and are easily adapted to new data.

However, there are disadvantages as well, such as:

– the danger of 'model overstraining'; the danger of reducing a complex reality too rigorously in order to fit it into a simulation model.
– the danger of not using the right empirical data.
– the danger of adapting a theory to computer language, to the possibilities of a computer. This danger is considerably reduced by the availability of a large number of computer languages.

In general it can be stated that simulation models offer a relatively clear, easy, fast, and cheap method of investigating complex theories.

Linguistic versus numerical simulation

There exist numerous simulation techniques, such as analogue computers or digital computer languages like SIMULA, CSMP, or DYNAMO. A factor common to all techniques is that they are numerical – the variables assume numerical values. However, the power of numerical simulation models as a method for modelling social processes has some serious limita-tions. To be able to use the mathematical techniques all quantities have to be defined exactly and they have to be measurable numerically. This holds good for both the variables and the relationships in the model. Every scientist knows from experience that this often raises difficulties. Take, for example, the problem of validity, reliability, and accuracy. The very existence of a theory of measurement may highlight this fact.

We believe that the main difficulty is caused by the requirement of numerical precision. The more precisely and exactly one wants to work, the more simplifications and approximations one has to introduce; hence the greater the gap between reality and the derived theory. One might state that (often) precision is complementary to reliability.

Having presented these general remarks about simulation models, we would like to add a few additional disadvantages of numerical simulation models:

– the danger of 'overstraining' the empirical data to meet the requirement of numerical precision.
– the danger of 'over-interpreting' the numerical results of the model.
– the danger of 'overstraining' all kinds of vague relationships, by making them exact relationships, usually by means of simplification, complexity reduction, and approximations.

One possible way to diminish the required amount of precision is to use linguistic variables instead of numerical values. Similarly, one might use linguistic relationships between variables instead of numerical relationships. We hope that such linguistic models will be more reliable and significant because they are much more approximate and less pretentious than the numerical ones.

The factual algorithm

A linguistic simulation has the same core of linguistic rules as the fuzzy logic controller, namely a set of fuzzy implications S:

if A_1 then B_1, else, if A_2 then B_2, else, ... if A_n then B_n

defined by

$$\mu_S(y, x) = \max_i \min [\mu_{A_i}(x); \mu_{B_i}(y)] \qquad i = 1, 2 ... n.$$

However, the basic difference from the control algorithm is that, instead of a non-fuzzy input and a required non-fuzzy output, this model has linguistic values for its input and should finish with a linguistic value as output. Because a linguistic value is defined as a fuzzy set (see Section 7.2 on linguistic variables), this means that the input to the algorithm is a fuzzy set instead of a degenerated, non-fuzzy, single value. Hence the compositional rule of inference applies:

$$\mu_{B'}(y) = \max_x \min [\mu_{A'}(x); \mu_S(y, x)]$$

so that the output is a fuzzy set B'. This fuzzy output set will generally not be equal to one of the linguistic values of the term-set of the particular linguistic variable.

What we need is a procedure which gives the fuzzy set B' a linguistic label. This is done by a linguistic approximation procedure. This heuristic search procedure generates the linguistic values of the term-set (by means of the generative grammar which defines the syntactic rules of the linguistic variable) and successively fits the fuzzy set B' to these values. The least sum of squares (or any other distance measure) can be taken as the criterion. The algorithm is illustrated in Figure 23.

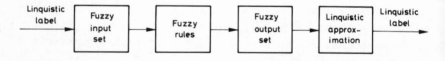

Fig. 23. Linguistic model structure.

To summarise, the flow diagram of the linguistic model (Figure 24) acts as follows: first we specify the linguistic variables by defining the primary values and syntactic rules. Then we specify the model structure by listing the linguistic rules. With this model and the initial values of the variables we can run the simulation loops.

Model of organisational behaviour

The first application of the linguistic simulation method described was the linguistic simulation of organisational behaviour reported in Wenstøp (1976). There this method was applied to model the findings of a case well known in organisational science, that of organisational behaviour at a mining company presented by Gouldner (1954). The dominant effect

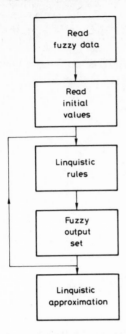

Fig. 24. Flow diagram of the linguistic model.

observed was an increased close supervision of the mineworkers. The result was an increase in bureaucratic rules and in the level of hostility towards supervisors, and a decrease in the workers' performance. In Gouldner (1954) a verbal model was constructed to explain the causes, effects, and the course of events. It was this model which was rephrased as a linguistic model in Wenstøp (1976). The structure of the causal relationships between the variables is shown in Figure 25.

The linguistic rules of the model were considered to be:

1. U_t becomes 'somewhat higher than' U_{t-1} (if L_{t-2} is 'very high' or 'rather high') or 'equal to' U_{t-1} (if L_{t-2} is 'not low' or 'very high') or 'slightly lower than' U_{t-1} (if L_{t-2} is 'low' or 'rather low').

2. K_t becomes 'very similar' to U_t.

3. L_t becomes 'very similar' to V_{t-1}.

4. D_t becomes 'similar to K_t (if L_t is 'not low') or 'similar to' L_t (if L_t is 'low' or 'sort of low' or 'rather low').

5. C_t becomes 'considerably higher than' C_{t-1} (if D_t is 'higher than' D_{t-1} and D_t is 'high') or 'equal to' C_{t-1} (if D_t is 'high' and D_t is 'not higher than' D_{t-1} or if D_t is 'not high or low') or 'slightly lower than' C_{t-1} (if D_t is 'low').

6. V_t becomes 'opposite of' U_t (if C_t is 'low' or 'rather low'), or 'very similar' to C_t (if C_t is 'not low').

7. V_t becomes 'equal to' V_{t-1} (if U_t is 'not higher than' U_{t-1}) or 'considerably lower than' V_{t-1} (if U_t is 'higher than' U_{t-1}).

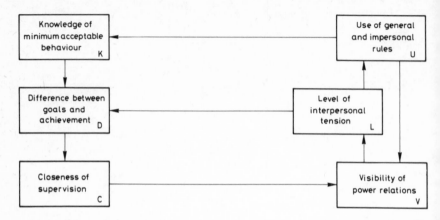

Fig. 25. The structure of causal relationships in Gouldner's model.

This model is used to answer questions on whether the linguistic model has the same behaviour as that actually observed, and on what the effects of different supervisory policies (other versions of rule 5) are in different situations.

After presenting nine simulations, Wenstøp (1976) comes to the following conclusions:

– the model corresponds well with Goudner's observations.

– high supervision produces high use of bureaucratic rules and low performance, no matter what the initial conditions.

– normal supervision leads to a high use of rules when starting from a favourable or unfavourable state, but does not change an intermediate state.

– there is no significant difference between the effect of normal or low supervision when starting from an intermediate or favourable state, but low supervision is the only policy that can change an unfavourable state into a more favourable one.

– a favourable state is untenable with any of the supervisory policies.

– it is probable that there does not exist a simple supervisory strategy which works well under all conditions.

In evaluating this method of verbal modelling, Wenstøp remarks that it has at least shown that verbal models can provide significant information, even though they are based on imprecision and intuition. He does not see much trouble in ensuring that the semantic model is representative of actual usage. One short-coming of the method is the lack of tools for mathematical analysis to supplement the simulation technique. However, as a pedagogic instrument for formal understanding of organisations by means of interactive computer simulation the technique may be very powerful.

Model of power theory

In Kickert (1976) a further application of the method is presented, namely a linguistic model of the social-psychological power theory of Mulder (1972). The reason for this particular choice was that a numerical simulation model of this theory also existed (Van Hezewijk et al. 1974). Moreover, this particular theory of power was presented in a rather unambiguous manner by means of 15 clear theses, which cannot be said of most social scientific theories. The outstanding characteristic of this theory is that it states that power itself can lead to satisfaction. Man strives for power, more power than he has. From this fundamental thesis Mulder proposes a theory about the reduction of the power-distance in a group. He conducted extensive laboratory and field experiments to confirm his theory. The theory is laid down in 15 theses which can be roughly divided into a group about the primary tendencies of people behaving in power situations (Theses one to five) and a group which describes secondary effects such as personality factors and crisis situations (Theses six to fifteen). All the theses are presented in Table 15.

Table 15. Mulder's fifteen theses.

Thesis 1   The exercise of power *per se* leads to satisfaction.
Thesis 2   The more powerful person strives to enlarge the power-distance in respect to the less powerful.
Thesis 3   This power-distance-increase tendency is stronger with a larger power-distance.
Thesis 4   The less powerful person strives for a reduction in power distance in respect to the more powerful.
Thesis 5   This power-distance-reduction is stronger with a smaller power-distance.
Thesis 6   A small power-distance is a satisfactory reason for the power-distance-reduction tendency.

Thesis 7   With a reduction of power-distance in reality the expected costs in-
            crease more than the benefits.
Thesis 8   In case of a very large power distance participation will not lead to a
            reduction but to an increase of the power-distance.
Thesis 9   The quantity of power (power distance) is a stronger determinant of
            p.d.r. than the quality, namely the legitimacy of power.
Thesis 10   In situations of crisis people need leaders who strongly exercise power.
Thesis 11   If leaders strongly exercise power, people credit them with a large
            self-confidence.
Thesis 12   People with a large amount of self-confidence and motivation for power
            show a stronger p.d.r. tendency.
Thesis 13   When less powerful people dispose of more self-confidence than the
            more powerful, their p.d.r. tendency in respect of those is larger.
Thesis 14   The p.d.r. tendency occurs in the Y-structure, even if people only
            imagine this structure and themselves in it.
Thesis 15   To equalize with another person is a human tendency, not restricted to
            the dimension of power. To be nice is infectious too.

From this set of theses a structural model of the causal relationschips has
been derived. Essentially thesis 1 means that we can model the theory as a
closed system. Theses 2 and 3 imply that we are dealing with a positive
feed-back loop in the power-distance increase, whereas theses 4 and 5
indicate a negative feed-back loop in the power-distance decrease. Thesis 7
was considered as a resistance factor in the tendency of power-distance
reduction. This resulted in the model illustrated in Figure 26.

Note that this models only a part of the power theory; the part of the theory
which accounts for personality factors is omitted. The rules used in the
linguistic power-distance reduction model are listed in Table 16.
These rules require somewhat more explanation. As will be clear from an
inspection of Table 16, we have used two rule structures in this model,
namely causal relationships of the forms:

1. If A is high then B is low.
2. If A is higher than B then C is lower than D.

Obviously two further alternative rule structures could be:

3. If A is high then B is lower than C.
4. If A is higher than B then C is low.

Another possible rule structure could be:

5. *A* is higher than *B*.

However, this last kind of rule no longer seems to be a causal relationship. The difficulty with these four different rule structures is that statements like 'the higher *A* the lower *B*' cannot be translated uniquely into one of these four rules. All four rules:

– if A_t is high then B_t is low,
– if A_t is high then B_{t+1} is lower than B_t,
– if A_{t+1} is higher than A_t then B_t is low,
– if A_{t+1} is higher than A_t then B_{t+1} is lower than B_t,

could be appropriate descriptions of this statement. The moral of this remark is that there evidently remains an interpretative danger with linguistics also (note that theses 3 and 5 of Mulder's power theory have this ambiguous form).

The result of several simulation runs shows that the model displays a stable character: the output tends to strive towards some 'golden mean' for nearly all situations. This is quite remarkable, because the results of the simulation model reported in Van Hezewijk et al. (1974) almost always showed an exponentially increasing, that is, a non-stable power-distance. This fact induced Kickert (1976) to consider different kinds of rules as well.

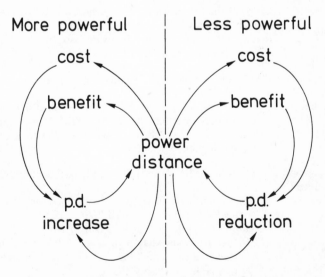

Fig. 26. Structural model of the power theory

Table 16. The rules of the power-distance-reduction model

Influence of power distance (PD) on power distance increase (PDI):
PDI_t becomes   'high' (if PD_t is 'high') or 'rather high' (if PD_t is 'rather high') or 'rather low' (if PD_t is 'rather low') or 'low' (if PD_t is 'low').

Influence of power distance (PD) on power distance reduction (PDR):
PDR_t becomes   'low' (if PD_t is 'high') or 'rather low' (if PD_t is 'rather high') or 'rather high' (if PD_t is 'rather low') or 'high' (if PD_t is 'low').

Influence of power distance (PD) on costs for the more powerful $(COSM)$:
$COSM_t$ becomes   'low' (if PD_t is 'rather low') or 'high' (if PD_t is 'rather high') or 'very high' (if PD_t is 'high').

Influence of power distance (PD) on benefits for the more powerful $(BENEM)$:
$BENEM_t$ becomes   'low' (if PD_t is 'rather low') or 'rather high' (if PD_t is 'rather high') or 'high' (if PD_t is 'high').

Influence of power distance (PD) on costs for the less powerful $(COSL)$:
$COSL_t$ becomes   'low' (if PD_t is 'rather high') or 'high' (if PD_t is 'rather low') or 'very high' (if PD_t is 'low').

Influence of power distance (PD) on benefits for the less powerful $(BENEL)$:
$BENEL_t$ becomes   'low' (if PD_t is 'rather high') or 'rather high' (if PD_t is 'rather low') or 'rather high' (if PD_t is 'low').

Influence of costs $(COSM)$ and benefits $(BENEM)$ on the power distance increase (PDI):
PDI_{t+1} becomes   'lower than' PDI_t (if $COSM_t$ is 'higher than' $BENEM_t$) or 'somewhat lower than' PDI_t (if $COSM_t$ is 'somewhat higher than' $BENEM_t$) or 'slightly lower than' PDI_t (if $COSM_t$ is 'slightly higher than' $BENEM_t$).

Influence of costs $(COSL)$ and benefits $(BENEL)$ on the power distance reduction (PDR):
PDR_{t+1} becomes   'lower than' PDR_t (if $COSL_t$ is 'higher than' $BENEL_t$) or 'somewhat lower than' PDR_t (if $COSL_t$ is 'somewhat higher than' $BENEL_t$) or 'slightly lower than' PDR_t (if $COSL_t$ is 'slightly higher than' $BENEL_t$).

Influence of power distance increase (PDI) and power distance reduction (PDR) on power distance (PD):
PD_{t+1} becomes   'lower than' PD_t (if PDR_{t+1} is 'higher than' PDI_{t+1}) or 'somewhat lower than' PD_t (if PDR_{t+1} is 'somewhat higher than' PDI_{t+1}) or 'similar to' PD_t (if PDR_{t+1} is 'similar to' PDI_{t+1}) or 'somewhat higher than' PD_t (if PDR_{t+1} is 'somewhat lower than' PDI_{t+1}) or 'higher than' PD_t (if PDR_{t+1} is 'lower than' PDI_{t+1}).

The rule structure of the first six blocks of rules was changed into the form

if X_t is high then Y_t is higher than Y_{t-1}.

Although the choice of this rule structure might look rather arbitrary, there was a reason for choosing it: one might see an intuitive similarity between the four kinds of rules and some kinds of differential, integral, or algebraic equations, For instance, a rule like 'if X_t is high then Y_t is higher than Y_{t-1}' might be considered the linguistic counterpart of the difference equation $Y_t - Y_{t-1} = K . X_t$. This second equation is the discrete counterpart of a differential equation:

$$d/dt \ Y(t) = \lim_{\Delta t \to 0} \frac{Y(t) - Y(t-1)}{\Delta t} = K'.X(t).$$

Hence the above-mentioned linguistic rule can be viewed as a linguistic integral equation of the form $d/dt \ Y \ (t) = K'.X \ (t)$.

In this same intuitive way one might argue that a rule of the form 'if X_t is higher than X_{t-1} then Y_t is high' represents a linguistic differential equation of the form $Y \ (t) = K'.d/dt \ X \ (t)$, and that a rule like "if X_t is high then Y_t is high" represents a linguistic algebraic equation of the form $Y \ (t) = K'.X \ (t)$.

However, we should be aware that there is no rigid mathematical basis for these analogies. This, of course, does not prevent the possibility that there might be a convincing practical basis for the analogies. Previous research on fuzzy logic controllers has indeed established some qualitative comparability between linguistic rules and differential, integral, and proportional equations (Kickert 1975). If this similarity actually holds, the change in rule structure of the first six blocks of rules in table 16 should result in a linguistic model which is almost the linguistic analogon of the system of differential equations used in the numerical simulation study of Van Hezewijk et al. (1974).

The results of runs with this simulation model have shown a tendency to become less and less informative with each iteration. On close inspection this fact is not so surprising; feeding a fuzzy input into a fuzzy relationship will result in a still more fuzzy output. Because of the iterative character of the model, a steady increase in fuzziness will occur. Of course, this kind of intuitive explanation does not prove anything.

Although to some extent this may be a reasonable and intuitively logical result, one cannot deny that it is rather annoying: it makes long-term predictions impossible. One might well be more interested in knowing what will happen in the long run, rather than in knowing what will happen in the very near future; it might be more interesting to predict that the power-distance will eventually become infinite than to predict that this distance will decrease during the first few steps. One could state that, by avoiding 'the danger of ever interpreting numerical results', we have now ended up with the complementary 'danger of the insignificance of linguistic results'.

Therefore, ways to reduce the fuzzification tendency were analysed in Kickert (1976). The most obvious way would be to sharpen the definitions of the consituent fuzzy sets and fuzzy relationships: by dimishing the spread of the fuzzy sets, their fuzziness will decrease. However, this would come down to the arbitrariness of the meaning of words, that is, the linguistic values. We do not think it sensible to shift and change these meanings at will.

A second possibility for decreasing the fuzziness in this linguistic system might be to adopt a different set of definitions for fuzzy logic. Although we have chosen a particular definition for fuzzy implication and fuzzy *modus ponens* (compositional rule of inference) many others are possible, as was shown in Section 7.3. The following combinations of definitions for fuzzy *modus ponens* $A * A \Longrightarrow B$ have been tried:

$$\mu_{A \Rightarrow B} = \max [1 - \mu_A; \mu_B]$$

with the minimum operator for $*$, and

$$\mu_{A \Rightarrow B} = \begin{array}{ll} \mu_B / \mu_A & \text{for } \mu_A \geq \mu_B \\ 1 & \text{otherwise.} \end{array}$$

with multiplication for $*$. Preliminary simulation tests have however indicated that none of these alternative definitions led to a decrease in the fuzziness of the simulation results.

A third possible way to reduce the fuzziness is to insert a transformation between successive model iterations. Instead of feeding the linguistic output value, or fuzzy output set, directly back into the next model iteration, the vague output dáta are first transformed into exact data before being again fed into the model. This is precisely the algorithm that has been proposed for fuzzy logic control. Certainly we are aware that this way of reducing the fuzziness in the model's results is no solution at all, but merely a rather artificial way of by-passing the problem. At every step vagueness is simply removed. This intermediate transformation of linguistic values into numerical values in fact touches the fundaments of this kind of model, namely the linguistic approach. Suffice it to give one counter-argument: it works.

The results of the simulation of this last type of model show that indeed the power-distance tends to explode, except when the initial distance is low. In this case it will tend to decrease further, even if it has an initial tendency to increase.

7.6. Discussion

In this last chapter the linguistic modelling approach has been discussed extensively. It has been shown that the method is based on two theories, the theory of linguistic variables and the theory of approximate reasoning, which have both been the subject of a relatively large number of theoretical studies. The theory of linguistic variables has extensively been studied in a number of papers by Zadeh. Fortunately these theoretical studies are supplemented by a series of empirical investigations into linguistic variables which we will discuss in the epilogue of this book.

The theory of approximate reasoning has also been extensively studied. The investigations by Gaines (1975, 1976 a, b) into the fundamentals of approximate reasoning – the logical systems underlying the theory – have revealed a lot of interesting properties. Surely in comparison to other fuzzy theories both these theories have quite extensively and intensively been investigated. It is a pleasant fact that these theoretical studies of the linguistic modelling approach are also supplemented in practical research. It has been argued that this approach, which enables one to model a process of which only a verbal description is possible, might be particularly suitable for the descriptive modelling of complex decision-processes. Fortunately these prophecies have not remained wishful thinking.

Numerous practical applications of this approach have been made in the field of process control, and a few applications have been made to the descriptive modelling of social systems. The usefulness of the method compared with the familiar numerical models has been demonstrated in some detail. The required precision and exactness of the latter often pose a huge and sometimes seemingly insurmountable problem. There is a great danger of 'overstraining' and 'overinterpreting' numerical data. More approximate, vague, and unpretentious linguistic data do not have these disadvantages.

It cannot however be denied that there remain a few question marks. As in most practical applications of fuzzy set theory, one of the main problems is how to obtain the particular fuzzy sets, and how to be sure that they represent the meaning of the linguistic terms. Wenstøp (1976) reported a method of finding acceptable meanings for primary terms through questionnaires. He also noted that people easily adapt to the slightly different use of natural language.

On the other hand, there are indications that the usual interpretation of meanings is not the one actually used in fuzzy sets. This semantical problem will be discussed in the epilogue.

It should be noted that the linguistic model requires a lot more computational effort than the corresponding numerical model, especially when numerical computer languages such as FORTRAN are used to programme the model.

A typical phenomeon that has been observed is that the linguistic model steadily increases the fuzziness of the results at every stage. Although intuitively speaking this seems right and evident, it prevents any possibility of long-term predictions. One possible pragmatic solution to this problem is to introduce a defuzzification step after each iteration. This has the additional advantage that it reduces considerably the required amount of computational time.

Another serious limitation of the linguistic modelling approach is that as yet there do not exist techniques for the mathematical analysis of a linguistic model. All the tools and techniques that are available to analyse the usual differential equation systems are totally absent here. It is clear that the method would greatly benefit from such analytical tools. Until now only the fuzzy logic controller type of linguistic model has been studied in this analytical sense.

Last but not least it should be emphasised that the question of the practical usefulness of the linguistic approach to descriptive decision-making models can only be answered by actual application of the method. Many more application studies will have to be carried out to study this question.

Epilogue

In the previous seven chapters we have discussed a wide range of theories from one-person, one-stage decision-making to sequential decision processes. Before turning to the final evaluation and conclusions of this survey, we would like to consider two questions which are fundamental to the whole of fuzzy set theory and which have not yet been specifically discussed, namely the problem of the semantics of fuzzy sets, (that is, how to ensure that the fuzzy sets used really represent the meaning that people attach to them), and secondly the methodological aspects of fuzzy set theory, (that is, what the methodology of science has to say about this new, rapidly advancing theory).

Semantics of fuzzy sets

One of the key problems which has been repeatedly noticed in the various theories is the problem of the determination and interpretation of the fuzzy sets that are used. In almost all the fuzzy theories that have been discussed the fuzzy sets were simply assumed to be given, and if not, some arbitrary examples of fuzzy sets were taken. Sometimes the particular examples of fuzzy sets that were used had very simple forms, such as linearly increasing forms or triangles, which cannot be said to be convincing from the point of view of their actual underlying meanings.

It is therefore reassuring that there exist a number of studies into the semantics of fuzzy sets. We will discuss these studies here in the following order: first a study into the question whether people actually do behave in a fuzzy set theoretic sense is considered. Then follows some consideration of studies with regard to their measurement aspects, and finally several studies which have investigated the semantics of two particular kinds of linguistics entities, namely hedges and the connectives 'and' and 'or'.

In Kochen (1975) the hypothesis that people do behave in accordance with the concept of degree of membership is supported by empirical evidence. It is studied whether people in a sample behave as statistical decision-makers using threshold decision criteria, or as fuzzy set theoretic actors with responses that vary continuously with the stimulus variable, that is, with a grade of membership. One out of two people seem to behave in the latter sense.

In most studies the actual grade of membership is determined by means of probabilistic methods. A question is asked of a number of people and the numbers of particular answers are determinant of the grade of membership (Kochen 1975; Kochen and Badre 1974; Hersch and Caramazza 1976; Rödder 1975). In Hersch and Caramazza (1976) this group interpretation of grade of membership is also compared to the experimental determination of individual grades of membership. In this latter experiment one subject is tested several times instead of testing several subjects once. Although several authors actually use much more sophisticated experimental tests than this rough description suggests, we feel that in a certain sense the problem of the differences between (subjective) probability and fuzziness – as touched on in the discussion of Chapter 1 – is reflected in the rather confusing use of probabilistic methods in the determination of fuzzy grades of membership. Remark that the use of a probabilistic method to construct fuzzy membership functions is quite distinct from the use of a statistical method to test hypotheses about fuzzy semantics, such as in Rödder (1975), where hypotheses about the form of the 'and' connective are tested. This distinction and many others that could be made emphasise that we have only roughly indicated the problem here. As stated before several authors use rather sophisticated experimental procedures. In Kochen and Badre (1974) semantic differentials are used, in Rödder (1975) a rank-ordering test is used, and Saaty (1974) even uses an eigenvalue method. In this latter method people are asked to indicate the amount to which one element x_i reveals a fuzzy property more than another element. This results in a judgement matrix $A = (a_{ij})$ of pairwise comparisons, $a_{ij} = w_i/w_j$ where the weights w_i are supposed to be the degrees of membership $\mu(x_i)$. The vector $w = (w_1, w_2, \ldots, w_n)$ can be recovered from the matrix A by finding the eigen vector of A for the maximum eigenvalue. This procedure, together with a basic scale of relative importances to determine the a_{ij}, completes the measurement procedure.

In Nowakowska (1977) the problem of the measurement of fuzzy concepts is studied. A structural formalism for the description of fuzzy concepts is presented and some remarks about possible procedures for the measurement of them are made. It is stated that measurement and scaling theory might provide the methodology for fuzzy measurement problems. Unfortunately the study remains very abstract and does not treat the above-mentioned confusion.

Apart from the more general studies into the semantics of fuzzy sets several studies into more particular fields exist, for instance into the semantics of hedges (Lakoff 1973, Kochen and Badre 1974, Hersch and Caramazza 1976) and the semantics of the connectives 'and' and 'or' (Rödder 1975, Hamacher 1975, Bellmann and Giertz 1973, Zimmermann et al. 1977).

The fuzzy set theoretic interpretation of linguistic hedges (see the footnote in section 7.2 on this term) such as 'very', 'rather', 'sort of' etc. presented by Zadeh (1972b) has triggered some studies into the semantics of these hedges (see Section 7.2). In Lakoff (1973) several hedges were investigated. It was shown that some fuzzy hedges require the assignment of vector values to the predicates they modify, that is, there are several meaning components of one predicate. Hedges apply in a structural way to these meaning components. Lakoff (1973) proposes a special fuzzy predicate logic with hedges to cope with these vector-values. Moreover it was argued that, in hedges such as 'sort of', 'rather', 'very' etc. algebraic functions such as proposed by Zadeh play a role. Whereas in Lakoff (1973) the study of linguistic hedges remained theoretical, in Kochen and Badre (1974), MacVicar-Whelan (1975); and Hersch and Caramazza (1976), linguistic hedges were empirically investigated. Kochen and Badre (1974) found that the linguistic hedge 'very' increases the slope of the membership function. Contrarily Hersch and Caramazza (1976) found that the hedge 'very' does not significantly influence the slope of the membership function but serves as a simple translation of the function along the abscissa. Unfortunately these contradictory results cannot be compared because of the different empirical measurement procedures used. Kochen and Badre (1974) use group averaged strengths of belief as membership values whereas Hersch and Caramazza (1976) use either group averages of binary answers or a mixture of individual time averages of binary answers with confidence levels as measures for their membership values. The interpretation of the hedge 'very' as a translation along the abscissa without change in slope is also supported by the experiments of MacVicar-Whelan (1975) who used a test procedure similar to that of Hersch and Caramazza (1976). Other results from the experiments of Hersch and Caramazza (1976) were that the definition of negation as the complement of a fuzzy set and the definition of 'or' as the union of two fuzzy sets were supported. Some people however were observed to interpret hedges in a different way, which was called 'linguistic interpretation'.

The other linguistic entities that have particularly attracted the interest of fuzzy researchers are the connectives 'and' and 'or'. In every elementary introduction these two connectives (together with the negation 'not') appear, and mostly they are defined as the union (minimum) and intersection (maximum) between two fuzzy sets respectively, according to the original definitions in Zadeh (1965a). Usually the choice of these definitions is considered arbitrary, but as long as they coincided with the classical set-theoretic definitions of union and intersection for binary truth values all definitions seemed right. In Bellman and Giertz (1973) an axiomatic formalism was presented from which it was proved that the minimum and maximum operators were the only possible for 'and' and 'or'. The formalism that was adopted was the following. Take the following notations:

$$\mu_{A \ and \ B} = f(\mu_A, \mu_B)$$

and:

$$\mu_{A \ or \ B} = g(\mu_A, \mu_B)$$

or in short notation:

$$f(x, y) = x \wedge y \text{ and } g(x, y) = x \vee y$$

Now assume the following conditions:

1. $\wedge$ and $\vee$ are commutative.
2. $\wedge$ and $\vee$ are associative.
3. $\wedge$ and $\vee$ are mutually distributive.
4. $x \wedge y$ and $x \vee y$ are continuous and non-decreasing in x.
5. $x \wedge x$ and $x \vee x$ are strictly increasing in x.
6. $x \wedge y \leq \min \{x, y\}$ and $x \vee y \geq \max \{x, y\}$.
7. $1 \wedge 1 = 1$ and $0 \vee 0 = 0$.

Then the only possible definitions are:

$$x \wedge y = \min \{x, y\} \quad \text{and} \quad x \vee y = \max \{x, y\}.$$

Although the seven axions in Bellmann and Giertz (1973) seemed quite natural, a study into the meaning that people attach to the connectives 'and' and 'or' revealed that the minimum definition of the logical connective 'and' was contradicted by experimental findings (Rödder 1975). These findings have initiated a series of studies at the same institute into the semantics of the 'and' and 'or' connectives. A theoretical study by Hamacher (1975) replaced the basic axioms of Bellman and Giertz (1973) with a more general axiomatic system. When the following axioms are assumed:

1. $\wedge$ is associative.
2. $\wedge$ is continuous.
3. $x \wedge y$ is injective in each argument x or y.
4. $x \wedge x = x \Longleftrightarrow x = 1$.
5. $x \wedge y$ is a rational function of x and y.

Then the definition has to be:

$$x \wedge y = \frac{x.y}{\gamma + (1-\gamma)\,(x + y - x.y)}$$

where $\gamma > 0$ and is an arbitrary parameter. If we arbitrarily choose $\gamma = 1$ then the definition simplifies to the product operator:

$$x \wedge y = x.y$$

Further empirical studies of Zimmermann et al. (1977) indicated that it might be useful to distinguish between two types of 'and', namely a 'logical and' and a 'compensatory and'. The concept of 'logical and' corresponds to the meaning of intersection in a set theoretic sense, e.g.:

transport-planes = planes $\cap$ means of transport.

For this type of purely logical 'and' the minimum operator seemed to be better supported by the empirical results than the product operator. The second type of 'and' corresponds to situations where negative aspects of one of the two components are compensated by positive aspects of the other, such as in the example:

an attractive car is fast 'and' beautiful,
while a not-so-fast but very beautiful car may still be attractive.

Empirical results from tests on this kind of 'compensatory and' better support the definition of geometric mean:

$$x \wedge y = \sqrt{x.y}$$

than definitions like arithmetic mean and minimum:

$$x \wedge y = (x + y)/2,$$
$$x \wedge y = \min \{x,y\}.$$

In conclusion, two major problems have emanated from our discussion of the semantics of fuzzy sets. First there is the problem of the use of probabilistic and statistical methods in the determination of fuzzy grades of memberships. It seems that considerations like that in Gaines (1976a: p. 186) where different measurement procedures are coupled to different systems of logic, might offer relief in unravelling the confusion. Secondly there is the problem of the multitude of incomparable measurement procedures, which, by the way, is quite common in social sciences. In our opinion a better view on the first mentioned problem will automatically solve the latter problem.

In view of the experimental determination of the degrees of membership that human beings attach to fuzzy concepts, it should be noted that algebraic studies of generalisations of fuzzy sets, such as the L-fuzzy set of Goguen (1967), offer some useful relief. For the essential result of these studies is that we do not have to restrict ourselves to a determination of degrees of membership which lie in the closed interval $[0, 1]$, but that any partially ordered set of degrees of membership will do. The only restrictions to this partially ordered set are that it should have a greater lower bound and a lower upper bound, and that it should possess distributivity. For example, this implies that non-comparability of two elements in their degree of membership is not excluded from the theory. This mathematical leeway should be compared with the strict assumptions underlying utility theory, namely that utility should be measured on an interval-scale at least.

Another important property that was emphasised in Gaines (1976b) is that approximate reasoning 'can do without the numbers'. Fuzzy logic can be treated axiomatically as a set of inference rules which applies to logical expressions in a many-valued logic. Of course fuzzy reasoning may also be carried out using numeric computation rather than symbolic processing, but this in no way detracts from its merits, since it does not rely on numerical operations and truth values.

We will conclude this section with a final remark about the semantics of fuzzy sets. In Section 7.5 we remarked that decision-making models could be divided into prescriptive and descriptive categories. In view of this distinction it should be clear that prescriptive models do not necessarily have to contain fuzzy sets, all of which describe how people actually behave, that is, prescriptive modelling does not necessarily have to bother about the semantics of all fuzzy sets, contrary to descriptive modelling which should indeed be totally based on it. An example of the difference between prescriptive and descriptive modelling right in the midst of the semantical studies of fuzzy sets is the difference between building an axiomatic formalism from which the definition of 'and' uniquely follows – a prescriptive model of the connective 'and' – and the empirical determination of the way that people interpret 'and' – a descriptive model of the connective 'and'. On the other hand it is clear that every prescriptive mathematical theory which is applied to solve real world problems should be based on a descriptive model of that real world. In this sense all fuzzy theories have to be concerned with the semantics of fuzzy sets.

Methodological questions

It is strange that, in spite of the interest that fuzzy set theory has attracted and the rather universal pretentions that the theory claims to have, no public methodological fight has yet broken out. The most probable reason is that the majority of the scientists who actually study the theory come from 'hard' sciences where methodological discussions are not so popular as in social sciences. Although we hesitate to introduce methodological discussions – methodological discussions very rarely reach a positive and final conclusion – we shall briefly touch on the subject here. Only three methodological criticisms will be mentioned here; no doubt real methodologists will be able to invent many more*.

Firstly it is a mistake to see reality as 'fuzzy'; it is the theories about reality that are fuzzy. The social sciences are not 'soft' because their objects are fuzzy, but because their theories are less precise, systematic, and abstract than the so-called 'hard' sciences. Hence fuzzy set theory may be a useful tool for imprecision in social theories, but not for the imprecision of 'reality'.

* I am grateful to R. van Hezewijk for having brought these points to my attention, although I am sure that he will still disagree with my opinions.

A second fallacy is the belief that fuzzy set theory is a new theory. Like all mathematics, fuzzy set theory is merely a language in which theories can be formulated. Fuzzy set theory is used to fuzzify theoretical propositions – this should not be confused with theories about the object 'language' such as the linguistic theories of Chomsky (1965) which is something quite different from constructing a new theory, that is, a set of universal statements. Theories are independent of any language in which these statements may be formulated (Popper 1959). It is the aim of science to produce better theories, theories with more universal content and more empirical content, theories which can better explain more empirical phenomena.

The language in which a theory is formulated is however not unimportant; the more specific or precise the language, the better the theory can be tested. For it is the testability of a theory, and the consequent possibility for its falsification, which determines the quality of a theory (Popper 1959). This is an argument in favour of numerical, precise languages and works at the expense of vague linguistic forms of language. The more specific, precise predictions can be made, the more testable the theory, and hence the higher the chances of falsifying it. This is what Popper calls a 'better theory'.

Our objection to this last argument is that this circumvents the fact that testing very precise predictions, which result from a very precisely formulated theory, without empirical data of the same precision does not seem to make sense. How can we test if we cannot measure? In our view the language in which a theory is formulated should correspond to the level of empirical testability, which seems to be the exact opposite of Popper's argument.

With regard to the second argument, I agree that so far fuzzy sets have mostly fuzzified theoretical propositions from existing theories, and are therefore just a new language. This does not alter the possibility that real 'new theories' based on fuzzy sets might eventually be found, and that is might well be because of the 'mere language' in which they are formulated. Scientific progress is unpredictable.

The first argument obviously needs some explanation because of its strangeness. The basic assumption behind this point is that reality *per se* does not exist; only models of reality exist (note that every observation of reality is in fact a model of reality). In this sense only models (or theories) can be fuzzy. On the other hand it is clear that there is nothing 'fuzzy' about fuzzy set theory, which is a precise mathematical theory. Therefore the argument looks quite strange, to put it mildly. In my opinion the argument does not imply more than that the statement should read 'fuzzy set theory is a tool for the vagueness of "observed reality"', which in the methodological sense is indeed a theory of reality and not reality itself. The conclusion that fuzzy set theory can only be a tool for the imprecision in social scientific theories is nonsense. As usual the practical implications of methodological criticism appear to be rather limited.

Conclusions

We cannot claim to have discussed thoroughly the applicability of fuzzy set theory to the modelling of decision-making in social systems. In order to do that we would firstly have to decide from the point of view of the social sciences which requirements should be satisfied and how to measure the performance of a fuzzy decision theory. We have not done that conscientiously. In the first part of this book we discussed the usefulness of fuzzy decision theories from the point of view of existing mathematical decision theories. Only in the second part did we briefly touch the problem of the usefulness of decision-making models. We have discussed the division into prescriptive and descriptive modelling and introduced linguistic modelling as a technique for the second of these. Even then we were not able to specify which particular problems, in which particular field of application, could or could not be handled with the various fuzzy decision theories. This implies. that the remarks about usefulness remained rather vague. Nevertheless, we believe that this critical survey of existing fuzzy theories has led to some judgement on the usefulness of all these theories.

We do not want to repeat here the remarks and conclusions about each specific theory – the relevant chapters can be referred to for specific conclusions – but only to present a few general conclusions:

– the fuzzy theories on decision- making which have been considered seem to have originated from the wish to apply fuzzy set theory rather than to have been invented or developed to solve specific practical problems.
– most fuzzy decision theories are straightforward extensions of the corresponding conventional theories.
– the techniques resulting from the fuzzy theories can often be reduced to well-known conventional techniques. This obviously offers a great computational advantage. Sometimes, however, the fuzzy theory is in fact identical to the corresponding conventional theory.

– it is a great pity that there exist only very few practical applications of fuzzy decision theories, and even practical examples to illustrate the theories are scarce.

– many fuzzy theories on decision-making seem to require even more precise definitions and analytical functions than the corresponding conventional theories.

– although it seems a dubious exercise to compare the various theories with each other, and even more dubious to choose among them, the linguistic approach looks rather appealing and promising.

To summarise, one might conclude that fuzzy set theory has indeed extended traditional mathematical decision theories so that they can cope with vagueness. In a methodological sense we can state that these theories have been extended to cope with a broader part of empiry; therefore we can speak of 'better theories'. On the other hand, these additional parts of empiry are nowhere specified, so that we might well state that the fuzzy theories are just as previous theories but merely formulated in a 'new language'.

Although the major part of this survey has been devoted to mathematical prescriptive decision theories and descriptive decision theories were only briefly discussed in the last chapter, we think that in the area of human decision-making, or decision-making in social systems where decision-making is not carried out in a mathematically rational way, fuzzy set theory has not yet shown its usefulness. It is yet our sincere conviction that fuzzy sets will eventually prove useful and applicable in these fields. The great barrier which seems to prevent rapid growth of fuzzy set research in this area is the ever-present gap between mathematics and social sciences. It is an absolute necessity that more social scientists become interested, convinced, and involved in this new theory so that they can actively support and direct the investigations of more mathematically orientated scientists. On the other hand, the 'hard' scientists should leave their home fields and penetrate into social science fields, but not as omniscient messiahs. In short, in this field, as in many others, there is a serious need for a synthesis between the 'hard' and 'soft' sciences.

Appendix: Basic definitions of the theory of fuzzy sets

Fuzzy set theory enables us to handle inexact, vague data and yet to work in a mathematically strict and rigorous way – vagueness is defined as a fuzzy set. Because the concept is defined on the level of set theory, which in fact constitutes the general fundament of the whole of mathematics, the theory of fuzzy sets is a rather universal theory. It was first introduced by Zadeh (1965a), who has since inspired most of the research done in this field.

In ordinary set theory, by definition, a set consists of a finite or infinite number of elements. The elements of one set's universe of discourse either belong or do not belong to the particular set. This is denoted by the characteristic function f_A of a set A. This function can only take the value 0 or 1. If the universe of discourse is $X = \{x\}$, then the characteristic function f_A of the set A becomes:

$f_A(x) = 1$ if and only if $x \in A$.
$f_A(x) = 0$ if and only if $x \notin A$.

Zadeh introduced the concept of fuzziness in set theory by generalising the characteristic function. This function is allowed to assume an infinite number of different values in the closed interval $[0,1]$. Elements belong to a fuzzy set with different grades of membership. According to Zadeh (1965):

Let the universe of discourse be $X = \{x\}$. A fuzzy set A on X is defined by its membership function $\mu_A(x)$ which assigns to each element $x \in X$ a real number in the interval $[0,1]$ where the value of $\mu_A(x)$ represents the grade of membership of x in A.

An ordinary set thus becomes only a special type of fuzzy set with a membership function which is reduced to the well-known two-value characteristic function.

Notation

Although strictly speaking a fuzzy set is just a mapping, namely the mapping from the support set (universe of discourse) into the closed interval [0,1], which implies that we should denote a fuzzy set A on X by its membership function:

$$\mu_A : X \to [0,1] \quad \text{or} \quad \mu_A(x), \ \forall x \in X$$

alternative notations are often encountered, for example:

$$A = \mu_1(x_1)/x_1 + \mu_2(x_2)/x_2 + \ldots \ldots \mu_n(x_n)/x_n$$

$$A = \sum_{i=1}^{n} \mu_A(x_i)/x_i$$

or in the continuous case:

$$A = \int_X \mu_A(x)/x.$$

By using the sum or integral sign to denote the union of all single membership values (rather than the arithmetic sum), these notations accentuate the false impression that a fuzzy set is a conventional set.

An example may help clarify the concept. In the fuzzy set $A = \{ \text{young} \}$ on the universe of positive integer numbers some of its membership functions may be:

$$\mu_A(0) = \mu_A(5) = \mu_A(10) = \mu_A(15) = \mu_A(20) = 1.0; \mu_A(25) = 0.9;$$
$$\mu_A(30) = 0.8; \mu_A(35) = 0.6; \mu_A(40) = 0.3; \mu_A(45) = 0.1; \mu_A(50)$$
$$= \mu_A(55) = ,\ldots, = 0.0$$

or the membership function may be represented by an analytical function such as (Figure A_1):

$$\mu_A(x) = (1 + (0.04x)^2)^{-1}.$$

A second example of a fuzzy set which stipulates its non-numerical character is the fuzzy set $A = \{\text{beautiful}\}$ where the universe consists of $X = \{\text{Mary, Betsy, Anne, Pamela}\}$. This fuzzy set might be defined as:

$$\mu_A(\text{Mary}) \quad = 0.7$$
$$\mu_A(\text{Betsy}) \quad = 0.6$$
$$\mu_A(\text{Anne}) \quad = 0.9$$
$$\mu_A(\text{Pamela}) = 0.3.$$

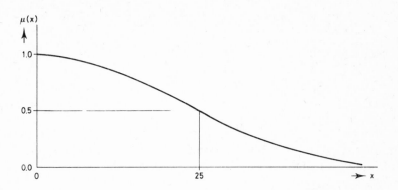

Fig. A1. The fuzzy set 'young'.

Because a fuzzy set is an extension of the concept of an ordinary set, it is not surprising that the basic definitions of fuzzy set theory, such as union, intersection, and complementation, are extensions of the corresponding definitions in ordinary set theory. All definitions of fuzzy sets coincide with those of ordinary sets in cases of only binary membership values (0 and 1).

This, however, leaves a lot of leeway. Take, for example, the definition of the union of two (ordinary) sets X and Y, denoted by $X \cup Y$:

$$x \in X \cup Y \quad \text{if} \quad x \in X \text{ or } x \in Y.$$

This definition can be translated in terms of the characteristic function:

$$f_{X \cup Y}(x) = \max\left[f_X(x); f_Y(x)\right]$$

or

$$f_{X \cup Y}(x) = f_X(x) + f_Y(x) - f_X(x).f_Y(x)$$

or any other function that satisfies Table A1.

Table A1. Tabular definition of union.

$f_{X \cup Y}$		f_X	
		0	1
f_Y	0	0	1
	1	1	1

By analogy the intersection of two sets $X \cap Y$ may be defined by means of the constituent characteristic functions, such as:

$$f_{X \cap Y}(x) = \min [f_X(x); f_Y(x)]$$

or

$$f_{X \cap Y}(x) = f_X(x) \cdot f_Y(x)$$

so long as Table A2 is satisfied.,

Table A2. Tabular definition of intersection.

$f_{X \cap Y}$		f_X	
		0	1
f_Y	0	0	0
	1	0	1

The definitions of union and intersection originally proposed and used since then are:

Union

The union of two fuzzy sets A and B on X, denoted $A \cup B$, is defined by

$$\mu_{A \cup B}(x) = \max \{\mu_A(x); \mu_B(x)\} \qquad\qquad x \in X$$

The union corresponds to the connective "or".

Intersection

The intersection of two fuzzy sets A and B on X, denoted $A \cap B$, is defined by

$$\mu_{A \cap B}(x) = \min \{\mu_A(x); \mu_B(x)\} \qquad\qquad x \in X.$$

The intersection corresponds to the connective "and".

Usually the max and min operators are abbreviated as $\vee$ and $\wedge$ respectively:

$$\mu_{A \cup B} = \mu_A \vee \mu_B$$
$$\mu_{A \cap B} = \mu_A \wedge \mu_B.$$

The third basic notion from set theory, namely the notion of complementation, has been extended to fuzzy complementation in the following way:

Complementation

The complement $\neg A$ (or $\bar{A}$) of a fuzzy set A is defined by

$$\mu_{\neg A}(x) = 1 - \mu_A(x) \qquad\qquad x \in X.$$

Complementation corresponds to the negation "not".

Obviously this is an extension of one of the arbitrary definitions of complementation in terms of characteristic functions. The concepts of union, intersection, and complementation are illustrated in Figure A2.

Algebraic properties

By using the abovementioned definitions for union, intersection, and com-

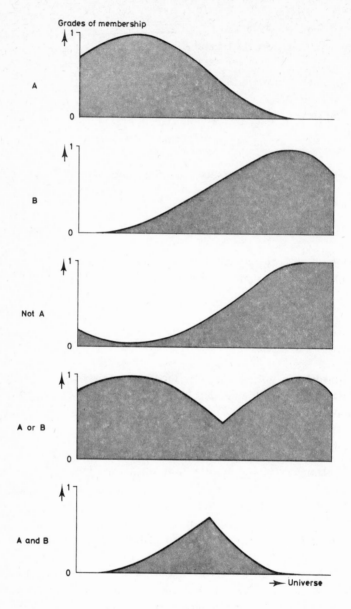

Fig. A2. Basic definitions of fuzzy sets

plementation, it is easily verified that many algebraic properties from ordinary set theory also hold good for fuzzy sets.

$$A \cap B = B \cap A$$

commutativity

$$A \cup B = B \cup A$$

$$(A \cap B) \cap C = A \cap (B \cap C)$$

associativity

$$(A \cup B) \cup C = A \cup (B \cup C)$$

$$A \cap A = A$$

idempotency

$$A \cup A = A$$

$$A \cap (B \cup C) = (A \cap B) \cup (A \cap C)$$

distributivity

$$A \cup (B \cap C) = (A \cup B) \cap (A \cup C)$$

$$(\overline{A}) = A$$ involution

$$\overline{A \cap B} = \overline{A} \cup \overline{B}$$

De Morgan theorems

$$\overline{A \cup B} = \overline{A} \cap \overline{B}$$

It is evident that the following properties of ordinary sets:

$$X \cap \overline{X} = \emptyset$$
$$X \cup \overline{X} = E$$

where

$$\emptyset : f_{\emptyset}(x) = 0 \quad \forall x \in X$$
$$E : f_E(x) = 1 \quad \forall x \in X$$

do not hold good for fuzzy sets. This represents the law of the excluded middle, whereas the concept of a fuzzy set is precisely the negation of that law. The following properties hold for fuzzy sets

$$A \cap \emptyset = \emptyset$$
$$A \cup \emptyset = A$$
$$A \cap E = A$$
$$A \cup E = E.$$

If we had taken the alternative definitions for intersection and union

$$\mu_{A \cup B} = \mu_A + \mu_B - \mu_A \cdot \mu_B$$
$$\mu_{A \cap B} = \mu_A \cdot \mu_B$$

the properties of distributivity and idempotence would no longer hold good.

We shall now present some additional definitions of fuzzy set theory.

Empty fuzzy set

A fuzzy set A on X is empty, denoted $\emptyset$, if and only if (iff) its membership function is equal to zero everywhere on X:

$$A = \emptyset \quad \text{iff} \quad \mu_A(x) = 0 \qquad \qquad \forall x \in X$$

Equal fuzzy sets

The fuzzy sets A and B on X are equal, denoted $A = B$, iff their membership functions are equal everywhere on X:

$$A = B \quad \text{iff} \quad \mu_A(x) = \mu_B(x) \qquad \qquad \forall x \in X$$

Containment

A fuzzy set A is contained in B (sub-set of B), denoted $A \subset B$, iff its membership function is less or equal to that of B everywhere on X:

$$A \subset B \quad \text{iff} \quad \mu_A(x) \le \mu_B(x) \qquad \qquad \forall x \in X$$

In Figure A3 the fuzzy set A is clearly contained in B.

So far we have considered fuzzy sets on one universe of discourse. The extension to multi-variate membership functions, that is to fuzzy relationships, is self-evident.

Fuzzy relation

Let X and Y be ordinary sets. The Cartesian product $X \times Y$ is the collection of ordered pairs (x, y), $x \in X$, $y \in Y$.

A binary fuzzy relation R from a set X to a set Y is a fuzzy sub-set on $X \times Y$,

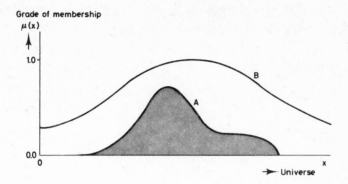

Fig. A3. An example of containment.

and is characterised by a two parameter membership function $\mu_R(x,y)$ in the interval $[0,1]$.

This is a quite straightforward extension of the ordinary relation which is defined as a sub-set of the Cartesian product of X and Y:

$$R \subset X \times Y.$$

More generally, a n-ary fuzzy relation is a fuzzy sub-set on $X_1 \times X_2 \times \ldots X_n$ characterised by its membership function:

$$\mu_R(x_1, x_2 \ldots x_n) \in [0,1] \qquad\qquad x_i \in X_i, i = 1, 2 \ldots n$$

An illustration of the concept of a fuzzy relation is the fuzzy relation 'resemblance'. Let the two universes of discourse X and Y be

$$X = \{ Tom, Dick \} \text{ and } Y = \{ John, Jim \}.$$

The binary fuzzy relation might then be expressed as a matrix:

$$
\begin{array}{c c}
 & \begin{array}{cc} \text{John} & \text{Jim} \end{array} \\
\begin{array}{c} \text{Tom} \\ \text{Dick} \end{array} &
\begin{bmatrix} 0.8 & 0.6 \\ 0.2 & 0.9 \end{bmatrix}
\end{array}
$$

where the (i,j) th element is the value of $\mu_R(x_i, y_j)$.

Another example of a fuzzy relation is the relation 'much larger than':

$x \gg y$ with $X = Y = R$. This fuzzy relation (Figure A4) may then be represented by an analytical function such as:

$$\mu_R(x,y) = (1 + (x-y)^{-2})^{-1} \qquad \text{if } x > y$$
$$= 0 \qquad \text{if } x \leq y.$$

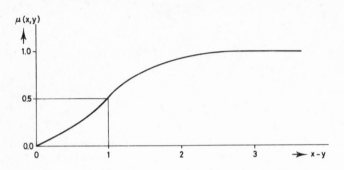

Fig. A4. The fuzzy relation 'much larger than'.

Composition of fuzzy relations

Let R_1 be a fuzzy relation from X to Y and R_2 a fuzzy relation from Y to Z. The composed fuzzy relation C from X to Z is written as $C = R_1 o R_2$ and defined by the membership function:

$$\mu_C(x,z) = \max_y \min \{ \mu_{R_1}(x,y); \mu_{R_2}(y,z) \} \qquad x \in X, y \in Y, z \in Z$$

or in short:

$$\mu_C = \bigvee_y (\mu_{R_1} \wedge \mu_{R_2}).$$

Suppose, for example, that we have two fuzzy relation matrices, one for the resemblance between { Tom, Dick } and { John, Jim }, and the other for the resemblance between { John, Jim } and { Phil, Mike }:

$$
\begin{array}{cc}
 & \begin{array}{cc} \text{John} & \text{Jim} \end{array} \\
\begin{array}{c} \text{Tom} \\ \text{Dick} \end{array} & \begin{bmatrix} 0.8 & 0.6 \\ 0.2 & 0.9 \end{bmatrix}
\end{array}
\quad \text{and} \quad
\begin{array}{cc}
 & \begin{array}{cc} \text{Phil} & \text{Mike} \end{array} \\
\begin{array}{c} \text{John} \\ \text{Jim} \end{array} & \begin{bmatrix} 0.3 & 0.8 \\ 0.5 & 0.7 \end{bmatrix}
\end{array}
$$

We can now compose the resemblance between { Tom, Dick } and { Phil, Mike } as follows:

$$\begin{bmatrix} 0.8 & 0.6 \\ 0.2 & 0.9 \end{bmatrix} \circ \begin{bmatrix} 0.3 & 0.8 \\ 0.5 & 0.7 \end{bmatrix} = \begin{bmatrix} 0.5 & 0.8 \\ 0.5 & 0.7 \end{bmatrix}$$

Shadow of a fuzzy relation

The shadow on X of a fuzzy relation R on $X \times Y$ is defined as a fuzzy set S on Y given by:

$$\mu_S(y) = \max_x \mu_R(x,y).$$

Cartesian product of fuzzy sets

Let A be a fuzzy set on X and B on Y; the Cartesian product of these fuzzy sets A and B is then defined by its membership function:

$$\mu_{A \times B} = \min \{ \mu_A(x) ; \mu_B(y) \}$$

with

$$X \times Y = \{ (x,y) | x \in X, \ y \in Y \}$$

being the definition of the classical Cartesian product. Note that, contrary to the definition of fuzzy intersection, this definition applies to two different universes of discourse.

Operations on fuzzy sets

It will be clear that we can define all kinds of operations which apply to the fuzzy membership function. One of them is the definition of the product of A and B, both on X, denoted by $A.B$:

$$\mu_{A.B}(x) = \mu_A(x) \cdot \mu_B(x) \qquad \forall x \in X.$$

A second one is the fuzzy set A^α where α is a positive number, which is defined by:

$$\mu_{A^\alpha}(x) = [\mu_A(x)]^\alpha \qquad \forall x \in X.$$

Similarly, the fuzzy set αA is defined by

$$\mu_{\alpha A}(x) = \alpha \mu_A(x) \qquad\qquad \forall\, x \in X.$$

These operations on fuzzy sets are used to represent linguistic hedges such as 'very', 'rather', 'more or less', etc. These linguistic hedges are seen as operating on the linguistic terms with which they are composed. Therefore, 'very young' would be an operation on the fuzzy set 'young'. Here we shall present briefly the basic operators on fuzzy sets that are used in the development of linguistic hedges.

Concentration

The concentration of the fuzzy set A on X, denoted CON(A), is defined by

$$\mu_{\text{CON}(A)}(x) = (\mu_A(x))^2 \qquad\qquad x \in X.$$

Dilation

The dilation of a fuzzy set A on X, denoted DIL(A), is defined by

$$\mu_{\text{DIL}(A)}(x) = (\mu_A(x))^{0.5} \qquad\qquad x \in X.$$

Note that

$$\text{CON}(A) \subset A \subset \text{DIL}(A).$$

Contrast intensification

The contrast intensification of a fuzzy set A on X, denoted by INT(A), is defined by

$$\begin{aligned}\mu_{\text{INT}(A)}(x) &= 2\,[\mu_A(x)]^2 &&\text{for} \quad 0 \leq \mu_A(x) \leq 0.5 \\ &= 1\text{-}2\,[1\text{-}\mu_A(x)]^2 &&\text{for} \quad 0.5 \leq \mu_A(x) \leq 1.\end{aligned}$$

This last operation differs from concentration in that it increases the membership function above 0.5 and diminishes it below 0.5. Notice that in all these operations the membership values zero and one are invariant values. Figure A5 illustrates the several operations discussed here.

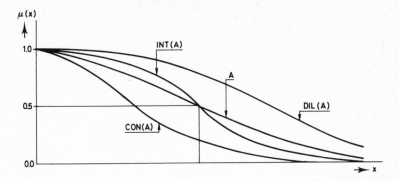

Fig. A5. Some operations on a fuzzy set.

One operation which differs in its working from those mentioned so far is the fuzzification operation, which operates on the support set of a fuzzy set. It transforms a non-fuzzy set into a fuzzy one or increases the fuzziness of an existing fuzzy set.

Fuzzifier

A fuzzifier F is characterised by its kernel $K(x)$, which is the fuzzy set resulting from the application of F to the element x. The result of applying F to a fuzzy set A is given by

$$F(A;K) = \int \mu_A(x)\, \mu_{K(x)}(x)/x.$$

As an illustration, assume that X, A, and $K(x)$ are defined by:

$$X = \{1, 2, 3\}$$
$$A = 0.8/1 + 0.6/2$$
$$K(1) = 1/1 + 0.4/2$$
$$K(2) = 0.4/1 + 1/2 + 0.4/3.$$

The fuzzification of A is then given by

$$\begin{aligned}
F(A;K) &= 0.8\,(1/1 + 0.4/2) + 0.6\,(0.4/1 + 1/2 + 0.4/3) \\
&= 0.8/1 + 0.32/2 + 0.24/1 + 0.6/2 + 0.24/3 \\
&= 0.8/1 + 0.6/2 + 0.24/3.
\end{aligned}$$

Linguistic hedges

By means of the above-mentioned operations on fuzzy sets we can define linguistic hedges such as 'very', 'plus', 'minus', 'more or less', 'slightly', 'sort of', 'rather', 'essentially', etc. (Zadeh 1972b).

Usually the linguistic hedge 'very' is interpreted as the concentration operation (Figure A6):

$$\text{very } A = A^2.$$

For example, if A = young, with

$$\mu_{\text{young}} = (1 + (0.04x)^2)^{-1}$$

then

$$\mu_{\text{very young}} = (1 + (0.04x)^2)^{-2}.$$

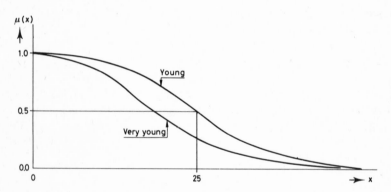

Fig. A6. The linguistic hedge 'very'.

The linguistic hedge 'rather' or 'more or less' may be defined by the dilation operation or by the fuzzifier operation.

With these definitions it is now possible to calculate the membership functions of such composite terms as:

$$x = \text{not very small and not large}$$
$$= (\neg(\text{small})^2) \wedge (\neg\text{large}).$$

Level set

The α-level set of a fuzzy set A on X is defined as the ordinary set S_α for which the degree of membership exceeds the level α:

$$S_\alpha = \{x \mid \mu_A(x) \geq \alpha\}. \qquad\qquad x \in X$$

This concept is illustrated in Figure A7.

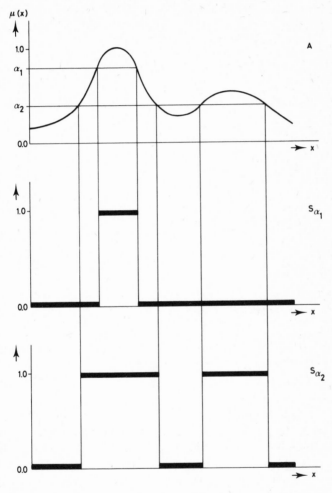

Fig. A7. Examples of level sets.

It is clear that the following property holds good for level sets:

$$\alpha_1 \geq \alpha_2 \quad \text{iff} \quad S_{\alpha 1} \subset S_{\alpha 2}.$$

Furthermore, we can prove that any fuzzy set can be decomposed into and composed from level sets, since:

$$A = \bigcup_{\alpha \in [0,1]} \alpha . S_\alpha$$

or

$$\mu_A(x) = \max_{\alpha \in [0,1]} [\alpha . \mu_{S_\alpha}(x)].$$

This is self-evident, because:

$$\mu_{S_\alpha} = 1 \text{ if } \mu_A(x) \geq \alpha$$
$$= 0 \text{ if } \mu_A(x) < \alpha$$

so that

$$\alpha . \mu_{S_\alpha} = \alpha \text{ if } \mu_A(x) \geq \alpha.$$
$$= o \text{ if } \mu_A(x) < \alpha.$$

Thus

$$\max_{\alpha \in [0,1]} [\alpha . \mu_{S_\alpha}(x)] = \max_{\alpha \leq \mu_A(x)} [\alpha] = \mu_A(x).$$

Of course, only in a case where there is a finite number of membership values can the fuzzy set be completely composed from a finite number of level sets.

This concludes the basic definitions of the theory of fuzzy sets. It should be noted that the particular choice of definitions made here remains arbitrary; this is not surprising in such a short introduction. We have tried to keep the number of definitions to a minimum in order to leave room for explanations and illustrations. We have restricted ourselves to the concepts that are used in the various chapters of this book. For an extensive treatment of the general theory of fuzzy sets the reader is referred to Kaufmann (1973), who gives a treatment at an introductory level, or to Negoita and Ralescu (1975), who treat the theory at a more algebraic level.

Bibliography

Arbib, M. A. (1977), Book reviews, in *Bulletin of the American Mathematical Society,* Vol. 83, No. 5, pp. 946-951.

Arbib, M. A. and E. G. Manes (1975), A category-theoretic approach to systems in a fuzzy world, in *Synthese* 30, pp. 381-406.

Arrow, K. J. (1951), *Social choice and individual values,* John Wiley, New York.

Asai, K. and S. Kitajima (1971), A method for optimizing control of multimodal systems using fuzzy automata, in *Information Sciences* 3, pp. 343-353.

Aubin, J. P. (1974a), "Théorie de jeux-coeur et valeur des jeux flous à paiements latéraux", *C. R. Acad. Sc. Paris,* t. 279, série A, pp. 891-894.

Aubin, J. P. (1974b), "Théorie de jeux-coeur et equilibres des jeux flous sans paiement latéraux", *C. R. Acad. Sc. Paris,* t. 279, série A. pp. 963-966.

Aubin, J. P. (1976), "Fuzzy core and equilibria of games defined in a strategic form", in *Directions in large-scale systems,* ed. Y. C. Ho and S. K. Mitter, Plenum Press, New York, pp. 371-388.

Baas, J. M. and H. Kwakernaak (1975), *Rating and ranking of multi-aspect alternatives using fuzzy sets,* Memorandum No. 73, Department of Applied Mathematics, Technical University of Twente, Enschede. Published (1977) in *Automatica* 13, pp. 47-58.

Bainbridge, L. (1975), "The process controller", in *The study of real skills,* ed. W. T. Singleton, Academic press, New York.

Bellman, R. E. and M. Giertz (1973), On the analytical formalism of the theory of fuzzy sets, in *Information Sciences* 5, pp. 149-156.

Bellman, R. E. and L. A. Zadeh (1970), Decision-making in a fuzzy environment, in *Management Science* Vol. 17 No. 4, pp. B-141-164.

Blin, J. M. (1974), Fuzzy relations in group decision theory, in *Journal of Cybernetics,* Vol. 4, No. 2, pp. 17-22.

Blin, J. M. and A. B. Whinston (1974), Fuzzy sets and social choice, in *Journal of Cybernetics,* Vol. 3, No. 4, pp. 28-36.

Boulding, K. E. (1962), *Conflict and defense, a general theory,* Harper and Brothers, New York.

Chang, S. K. (1971), Fuzzy programs-theory and applications, in Proc. of the symposium on computers and automata, Polytechnic Institute of Brooklyn Press, Vol. 21, pp. 147-164.

Chang, S. K. (1972), On the execution of fuzzy programs using finite state machines, in *IEEE trans. on computers,* Vol. 21, No. 3, pp. 241-253.

Chang, S. S. L. (1969), *Fuzzy dynamic programming and the decision-making process,* in Proc. of the third Princeton conference on information science and systems, pp. 200-203.

Chomsky, N. (1965), *Aspects of the theory of syntax,* M.I.T. Press, Cambridge, Mass.

Cohen, K. J. and R. M. Cyert (1965), Simulation of organizational behaviour, in *Handbook of organizations,* ed. J. G. March, Rand McNally, Chicago.

Cohen, M. D., J. G. March, and J. P. Olsen (1972), A garbage can model of organizational choice, in *Adm. Sci. Qu.,* Vol. 17, No. 1, pp. 1-25.

176   BIBLIOGRAPHY

Cyert, R. M., E. A. Feigenbaum, and J. G. March (1959), Models in a behavioural theory of the firm, in *Behavioural Science*, Vol. 4, pp. 81-95.

Cyert, R. M. and J. G. March (1963), *A behavioral theory of the firm*, Prentice-Hall, Englewood Cliffs.

Edwards, W. (1954), The theory of decision-making, in *Psychological Bulletin*, Vol. 51, No. 4, pp. 380-417.

Van Eeden, D. (1976), *Fuzzy random variables in decision problems*, thesis, Department of Applied Mathematics, Technical University of Twente, Enschede.

Ferguson, T. S. (1967), *Mathematical statistics, a decision theoretical approach*, Academic Press, New York.

Fishburn, P. C. (1964), *Decision and value theory*, John Wiley, New York.

Fishburn, P. C. (1970), *Utility theory for decision-making*, John Wiley, New York.

Fung, L. W. and K. S. Fu (1975), An axiomatic approach to rational decision-making in a fuzzy environment, in Zadeh et al. (1975), pp. 227-256.

Gaines, B. R. (1975), Stochastic and fuzzy logics, in *Electronic Letters*, Vol. 11, No. 9, pp. 188-189.

Gaines, B. R. (1976a), *Fuzzy reasoning and the logics of uncertainty*, in Proc. of the sixth symp on multiple valued logic, Utah, IEEE 76 CH, 1111-4C,pp. 179-188.

Gaines, B. R. (1976b), Foundations of fuzzy reasoning, in *Int. J. Man-Machine Studies*, Vol. 8, pp. 623-668.

Gaines, B. R. and L. J. Kohout (1977), A bibliography of fuzzy systems and closely related topics, in *Int. J. Man-Machine Studies*, Vol. 9, pp. 1-68.

Gluss, B. (1973), Fuzzy multistage decision-making, fuzzy state and terminal regulators and their relationship to non-fuzzy quadratic state and terminal regulators, in *International Journal of Control*, Vol. 17, No. 1, pp. 177-192.

Goguen, J. A. (1967), L-fuzzy sets, in *Journal of Mathematical Analysis and Application*, Vol. 18, pp. 145-174.

Goguen, J. A. (1969), The logic of inexact concepts, in *Synthese*, Vol. 19, Nos. 3/4, pp. 325-373.

Gouldner, A. W. (1954), *Patterns of industrial bureaucracy*, The Free Press, Glencoe, Ill.

Hamacher, H. (1975), *über logische Verknüpfungen unscharfer Aussagen und dehren zugehörige Bewertungsfunktionen*, Rep. 75/14, RWTH Aachen.

Harbordt, S. (1974), *Computer Simulation in der Sozialwissenschaften*, Rowohlt, Reinbek.

Hersch, H. M. and A. Caramazza, (1976), A fuzzy set approach to modifiers and vagueness in natural language, in *Journal of Experimental Psychology: General*, Vol. 105, No. 3, pp. 254-276.

Van Hezewijk, R., H. Kanters, and A, Melief (1974), Playing the game of power, in *Annals of Systems Research*, Vol. 4, pp. 39-60.

Jain, R. (1976), Decision-making in the presence of fuzzy variables, in *IEEE transactions on system, man, and cybernetics*, October 1976, pp. 698-703.

Jain, R. (1977), A procedure for multi-aspect decision-making using fuzzy sets, in *Int. J. Systems Sci.*, Vol. 8, No. 1, pp. 1-7.

Kahne, S. (1975), A contribution to decision-making in environmental design, in *Proc. IEEE*, Vol. 63, No. 3, pp. 518-528.

Kaufmann, A. (1973), *Introduction à la théorie des sous-ensembles flous. Thome 1: Elements théorique de base*, Masson, Paris. (Also available as *Introduction to the theory of fuzzy sub-sets*, Academic Press, New York, 1975).

Kaufmann, A. (1975a), *Introduction à la théorie des sous-ensembles flous. Thome 2: Applications à la linguistique, à la logique et à la sémantique*, Masson, Paris.

Kaufmann, A. (1975b), *Introduction à la théorie des sous-ensembles flous. Thome 3: Applications à la classification et à la reconnaissance des formes, aux automates et aux systèmes, aux choix des critères*, Masson, Paris.

Kaufmann, A. (1977), *Introduction à la théorie des sous-ensembles flous. Thome 4: Compléments et nouvelles applications*, Masson, Paris.

Kickert, W. J. M. (1975), *Further analysis and application of fuzzy logic control*, Intern. Report No. F/WK2/75, Department of Electrical Engineering, Queen Mary College, London.

Kickert, W. J. M. (1976), An example of linguistic modelling, Int. Report 30, Department of Industrial Engineering, Techn. University of Eindhoven to appear in *Annals of Systems Research*. 1978.

Kickert, W. J. M. and H. Koppelaar (1976): Application of fuzzy set theory to syntactic pattern recognition of handwritten capitals, *IEEE transactions on Systems, Man and Cybernetics*, Vol. 6, pp. 148-151.

Kickert, W. J. M. and E. H. Mamdani (1978), Analysis of a fuzzy logic controller, in *Fuzzy Sets and Systems*, Vol. 1, No. 1, pp. 29-44.

Kickert, W. J. M. and H. R. van Nauta Lemke (1976), Application of a fuzzy controller in a warm water plant, in *Automatica*, Vol. 12, pp. 301-308.

King, P. J. and E. H. Mamdani (1975), *The application of fuzzy control systems to industrial processes*, in special interest discussion session on fuzzy automata and decision processes, sixth IFAC world congress, Boston, Mass.

Kling, R. (1974), Fuzzy planner: reasoning with inexact concepts in a procedural problem-solving language, in *Journal of Cybernetics*, Vol. 3, No. 4, pp. 1-16.

Kochen, M. (1975), Applications of fuzzy sets in psychology, in Zadeh et al. (1975) pp. 395-408.

Kochen, M. and A. N. Badre (1974), On the precision of adjectives which denote fuzzy sets, in *Journal of Cybernetics*, Vol. 4, No. 1, pp. 49-59.

Lakoff, G. (1973), Hedges: a study in meaning criteria and the logic of fuzzy concepts, in *Journal of Philosophical Logic*, Vol. 2, pp. 450-508.

Lee, R. C. T. (1972), Fuzzy logic and resolution principle, in *Journal of the Association for Computing Machinery*, Vol. 19, pp. 109-119.

Lehman, E. L. (1959), *Testing statistical hypotheses*, John Wiley, New York.

Luce, R. D. and H. Raiffa (1957), *Games and decisions*, John Wiley, New York.

MacVicar-Whelan, P. J. (1974), Fuzzy sets, the concept of height and the hedge 'very', Technical Memorandum 1, Physics Department, Grand Valley State Colleges, Allendale, Michigan.

Mamdani, E. H. (1974), Applications of fuzzy algorithms for control of simple dynamic plant, in *Proc. IEE*, Vol. 121, No. 12, pp. 1585-1588.

Mamdani, E. H. (1976), Advances in the linguistic synthesis of fuzzy controllers, in *Int. J. of Man-Machine Studies*, Vol. 8, pp. 669-678.

Mamdani, E. H. and S. Assilian (1975), An experiment in linguistic synthesis with a fuzzy logic controller, in *Int. J. Man-Machine Studies*, Vol. 7, pp. 1-13.

March, J. G. and H. A. Simon (1958), *Organizations*, J. Wiley, New York.

Marschak, J. and R. Radner (1972), *Economic theory of teams*, Yale University Press.

Mintzberg, H., D. Raisinghani, and A. Theoret (1976), The structure of 'unstructured' decision processes, in *Adm. Sci. Qu.*, Vol. 21, pp. 246-275.

Mizumoto, M., J. Toyoda, and K. Tanaka (1969), Some considerations on fuzzy automata, in *Journal of Computer and System Sciences*, Vol. 3, pp. 409-422.

Mulder, M. (1972), *Het spel om de macht*, Boom, Meppel.

Nasu, M. and Honda N. (1968), Fuzzy events realized by finite probabilistic automata, in *Information and Control*, Vol. 12, pp. 284-303.

Van Nauta Lemke, H. R. and W. J. M. Kickert (1976), The application of fuzzy set theory to control a warm water process, in *Journal A*, Vol. 17, No 1, pp. 8-18, Belgium/the Netherlands.

Negoita, C. V., S. Minoiu, and E. Stan (1976), On considering imprecision in dynamic linear programming, in *ECECSR Journal*, Vol. 3, pp. 83-95.

Negoita, C. V. and D. A. Ralescu (1974), Fuzzy systems and artificial intelligence, in *Kybernetes*, Vol. 3, pp. 173-178.

Negoita, C. V. and D. A. Ralescu (1975), *Applications of fuzzy sets to systems analysis*, Birkhauser, Basel.

Negoita, C. V. and A. C. Stefanescu (1975), On the state equation of fuzzy systems, in *Kybernetes*, Vol. 4, pp. 213-214.

Negoita, C. V. and M. Sularia (1976), On fuzzy mathematical programming and tolerances in planning, in *ECECSR Journal*, Vol. 1, pp. 3-14.

Von Neumann, J. and O. Morgenstern (1944), *Theory of games and economic behaviour*, Princeton University Press, Princeton.

Newell, A. and H. A. Simon (1972), *Human problem solving*, Prentice-Hall, Englewood Cliffs.

Nowakowska, M. (1977), methodological problems of measurement of fuzzy concepts in the social sciences, in *Behavioral Science*, Vol. 22, pp. 107-115.

Popper, K. R. (1959), *The logic of scientific discovery*, Hutchinson, London.

Rescher, N. (1969), *Many-valued logic*, McGraw-Hill, New York.

Rödder, W. (1975), *on 'and' and 'or' connectives in fuzzy set theory*, Working paper 75/07, RWTH Aachen. (Presented at EURO I, Brussels, 1975.)

Rödder, W. and H.-J. Zimmermann (1977), Analyse, Beschreibung und Optimierung von unscharf formulierten Problemen, in *Zeitschrift für Operations Research*, Vol. 22, pp. 1-18

Roy, B. (1975), *Partial preference analysis and decision-aid: the fuzzy outranking relation concept*, paper presented at the IIASA workshop 'Decision-making with multiple conflicting objects', Vienna.

Saaty, T. L. (1974), Measuring the fuzziness of sets, in *Journal of Cybernetics*, Vol. 4, No. 4, pp. 53-61.

Santos, E. S. (1968), Maximum automata, in *Information and Control* Vol. 13, pp. 363-377.

Santos, E. S. (1970), Fuzzy algorithms, in *Information and Control* Vol. 17, pp. 326-339.

Simon, H. A. (1947), *Administrative behaviour*, Macmillan, New York.

Stallings, W. (1977), Fuzzy set theory versus Bayesian statistics, in *IEEE trans. on systems, man and cybernetics*, Vol. 7 No. 3, pp. 216-219.

Tanaka, H., T. Okuda, and K. Asai (1974), On fuzzy mathematical programming, in *Journal of Cybernetics*, Vol. 3, No. 4, pp. 37-46.

Tanaka, H., T. Okuda, and K. Asai (1976), A formulation of fuzzy decision problems and its application to an investment problem, in *Kybernetes*, Vol. 5, pp. 25-30.

Tong, R. M. (1976), Analysis of fuzzy control algorithms using the relation matrix, in *International Journal of Man-Machine Studies*, Vol. 8, pp. 679-686.

Tong, R. M. (1977), A control engineering review of fuzzy systems, in *Automatica*, Vol. 13, pp. 559-569.

Van Velthoven, G. (1975), *Fuzzy models in personnel management*, paper presented at third Int. Congress of Cybern. and Systems, Bucharest.

Vincke, P. (1973), Une application de la théorie des graphes flous, in *Cahiers du centre d'études de recherche operationelle*, Vol. 15, No. 3. pp. 375-395.

Wald, A. (1950), *Statistical decision functions*, John Wiley, New York.

Wee, W. G. and K. S. Fu (1969), A formulation of fuzzy automata and its application as a model of learning systems, in *IEEE trans. on systems, science, and cybernetics*, Vol. 5, No. 3, pp. 215-223.

Wenstøp, F. (1976), Deductive verbal models of organizations, in *International Journal of Man-Machine Studies*, Vol. 8, pp. 293-311.

Yager, R. R. (1977), Multiple objective decision-making using fuzzy sets, *International Journal of Man-Machine Studies*, Vol. 9, pp. 375-382.

Zadeh, L. A. (1965a) Fuzzy sets, in *Information and Control*, Vol. 8, pp. 338-353.

Zadeh, L. A. (1965b), *Fuzzy sets and systems,* in proc. of symposium on system theory, Polytechn. Inst. of Brooklyn, pp. 29-37.

Zadeh, L. A. (1968), Probability measures of fuzzy events, in *J. Math. Anal. Appl.,* Vol. 23, pp. 421-427.

Zadeh, L. A. (1969), *Towards a theory of fuzzy systems,* in Techn. Report ERL-69-2, Electr. Research Lab., University of California, Berkeley. Published in *Aspects of Networks and Systems Theory,* 1971, Holt, Rinehart and Winston, New York.

Zadeh, L. A. (1971), Similarity relations and fuzzy orderings, in *Information Sciences,* Vol. 3, pp. 171-200.

Zadeh, L. A. (1972a), *A system theoretic view of behaviour modification,* Memorandum ERL-M320, Electr. Research Lab, Iniv. of Calif., Berkeley.

Zadeh, L. A. (1972b), A fuzzy set interpretation of linguistic hedges, in *Journal of Cybernetics,* Vol. 2, No. 3, pp. 4-34.

Zadeh, L. A. (1972c), *Fuzzy languages and their relation to human and machine intelligence,* in proc. of Int. Conf. on man and computer, Basel, S. Karger, pp. 130-165.

Zadeh, L. A. (1973), Outline of a new approach to the analysis of complex system and decision processes, in *IEEE trans. on systems, man, and cybernetics,* Vol. 3, No. 1, pp. 28-44.

Zadeh, L. A. (1975a), The concept of a linguistic variable and its application to approximate reasoning, part I, in *Information Sciences,* Vol. 8, pp. 199-249; Part II in *Information Sciences,* Vol. 8, pp. 301-357; Part III in *Information Sciences,* Vol. 9, pp. 43-80.

Zadeh, L. A. (1975b), Fuzzy logic and approximate reasoning, in *Synthese,* Vol. 30, pp. 407-428.

Zadeh, L. A., (1976), A fuzzy algorithmic approach to the definition of complex or imprecise concepts, in *International Journal of Man-Machine Studies,* Vol. 8, pp. 249-291.

Zadeh, L. A., K. S. Fu, K. Tanaka, and M. Shimura (1975), *Fuzzy sets and their applications to cognitive and decision processes,* (proc. of the U.S./Japan seminar on fuzzy sets and their applications, Univ. of Calif., Berkeley, 1974), Academic Press, New York.

Zimmermann, H.-J. (1976), Description and optimization of fuzzy systems, in *Int. J. General Systems,* Vol. 2, pp. 209-215.

Zimmermann, H.-J. (1978), fuzzy programming and linear programming with several objective functions, in *Fuzzy Sets and Systems,* Vol. 1, No. 1, pp. 45-56.

Zimmermann, H.-J. et al. (1977), *Results of empirical studies in fuzzy set theory,* paper presented at International Conference on Applied General Systems Research, Binghampton, N.J., August 15-19, 1977.

Subject Index